Seattle Mariners 2020

A Baseball Companion

Edited by R.J. Anderson, Craig Goldstein and Bret Sayre

Baseball Prospectus

Craig Brown, Steven Goldman and David Pease, Consultant Editors
Robert Au, Harry Pavlidis and Amy Pircher, Statistics Editors

Copyright © 2020 by DIY Baseball, LLC.
All rights reserved

This book or any part thereof may not be reproduced or transmitted in any form or by any means, electronic or mechanical, including photocopying, recording, or by any information storage and retrieval system, without permission in writing from the publisher.

Limit of Liability/Disclaimer of Warranty: While the publisher and the author have used their best efforts in preparing this book, they make no representations or warranties with respect to the accuracy or completeness of the contents of this book and specifically disclaim any implied warranties of merchantability or fitness for a particular purpose. No warranty may be created or extended by sales representatives or written sales materials. The advice and strategies contained herein may not be suitable for your situation. You should consult with a professional where appropriate. Neither the publisher nor the author shall be liable for any loss of profit or any other commercial damages, including but not limited to special, incidental, consequential, or other damages.

Library of Congress Cataloging-in-Publication Data:
paperback
ISBN-13: 978-1-949332-86-5

Project Credits
Cover Design: Michael Byzewski at Aesthetic Apparatus
Interior Design and Production: Jeff Pease, Dave Pease
Layout: Jeff Pease, Dave Pease

Baseball icon courtesy of Uberux, from https://www.shareicon.net/author/uberux

Ballpark diagram courtesy of Lou Spirito/THIRTY81 Project, https://thirty81project.com/

Manufactured in the United States of America
10 9 8 7 6 5 4 3 2 1

Table of Contents

Statistical Introduction v

Part 1: Team Analysis

Seattle Mariners: Where Are You Going, Where Have You Been? 3
    Jeffrey Paternostro, Jen Mac Ramos and Matthew Trueblood

Performance Graphs 7

2019 Team Performance 8

2020 Team Projections 9

Team Personnel 10

T-Mobile Park Stats 11

Mariners Team Analysis 13

Part 2: Player Analysis

Mariners Player Analysis 18

Mariners Prospects 93

Part 3: Featured Articles

The Baseball Is Juiced (Again) 109
    Robert Arthur

The Moral Hazard of Playing It Safe 113
    Craig Goldstein

Index of Names 119

Statistical Introduction

Sports are, fundamentally, a blend of athletic endeavor and storytelling. Baseball, like any other sport, tells its stories in so many ways: in the arc of a game from the stands or a season from the box scores, in photos, or even in numbers. At Baseball Prospectus, we understand that statistics don't replace observation or any of baseball's stories, but complement everything else that makes the game so much fun.

What stats help us with is with patterns and precision, variance and value. This book can help you learn things you may not see from watching a game or hundred, whether it's the path of a career over time or the breadth of the entire MLB. We'd also never ask you to choose between our numbers and the experience of viewing a game from the cheap seats or the comfort of your home; our publication combines running the numbers with observations and wisdom from some of the brightest minds we can find. But if you *do* want to learn more about the numbers beyond what's on the backs of player jerseys, let us help explain.

Offense

We've revised our methodology for determining batting value. Long-time readers of the book will notice that we've retired True Average in favor of a new metric: Deserved Runs Created Plus (DRC+). Developed by Jonathan Judge and our stats team, this statistic measures everything a player does at the plate–reaching base, hitting for power, making outs, and moving runners over–and puts it on a scale where 100 equals league-average performance. A DRC+ of 150 is terrific, a DRC+ of 100 is average and a DRC+ of 75 means you better be an excellent defender.

DRC+ also does a better job than any of our previous metrics in taking contextual factors into account. The model adjusts for how the park affects performance, but also for things like the talent of the opposing pitcher, value of different types of batted-ball events, league, temperature and other factors. It's able to describe a player's expected offensive contribution than any other statistic we've found over the years, and also does a better job of predicting future performance as well.

There's a lot more to DRC+'s story, and you can read all about it in greater depth near the end of this book.

Seattle Mariners 2020

The other aspect of run-scoring is baserunning, which we quantify using Baserunning Runs. BRR not only records the value of stolen bases (or getting caught in the act), but also accounts for all the stuff that doesn't show up on the back of a baseball card: a runner's ability to go first to third on a single, or advance on a fly ball.

Defense

Where offensive value is *relatively* easy to identify and understand, defensive value is...not. Over the past dozen years, the sabermetric community has focused mostly on stats based on zone data: a real-live human person records the type of batted ball and estimated landing location, and models are created that give expected outs. From there, you can compare fielders' actual outs to those expected ones. Simple, right?

Unfortunately, zone data has two major issues. First, zone data is recorded by commercial data providers who keep the raw data private unless you pay for it. (All the statistics we build in this book and on our website use public data as inputs.) That hurts our ability to test assumptions or duplicate results. Second, over the years it has become apparent that there's quite a bit of "noise" in zone-based fielding analysis. Sometimes the conclusions drawn from zone data don't hold up to scrutiny, and sometimes the different data provided by different providers don't look anything alike, giving wildly different results. Sometimes the hard-working professional stringers or scorers might unknowingly inflict unconscious bias into the mix: for example good fielders will often be credited with more expected outs despite the data, and ballparks with high press boxes tend to score more line drives than ones with a lower press box.

Enter our Fielding Runs Above Average (FRAA). For most positions, FRAA is built from play-by-play data, which allows us to avoid the subjectivity found in many other fielding metrics. The idea is this: count how many fielding plays are made by a given player and compare that to expected plays for an average fielder at their position (based on pitcher ground ball tendencies and batter handedness). Then we adjust for park and base-out situations.

When it comes to catchers, our methodology is a little different thanks to the laundry list of responsibilities they're tasked with beyond just, well, catching and throwing the ball. By now you've probably heard about "framing" or the art of making umpires more likely to call balls outside the strike zone for strikes. To put this into one tidy number, we incorporate pitch tracking data (for the years it exists) and adjust for important factors like pitcher, umpire, batter and home-field advantage using a mixed-model approach. This grants us a number for how many strikes the catcher is personally adding to (or subtracting from) his pitchers' performance...which we then convert to runs added or lost using linear weights.

Framing is one of the biggest parts of determining catcher value, but we also take into account blocking balls from going past, whether a scorer deems it a passed ball or a wild pitch. We use a similar approach—one that really benefits from the pitch tracking data that tells us what ends up in the dirt and what doesn't. We also include a catcher's ability to prevent stolen bases and how well they field balls in play, and *finally* we come up with our FRAA for catchers.

Pitching

Both pitching and fielding make up the half of baseball that isn't run scoring: run prevention. Separating pitching from fielding is a tough task, and most recent pitching analysis has branched off from Voros McCracken's famous (and controversial) statement, "There is little if any difference among major-league pitchers in their ability to prevent hits on balls hit in the field of play." The research of the analytic community has validated this to some extent, and there are a host of "defense-independent" pitching measures that have been developed to try and extract the effect of the defense behind a hurler from the pitcher's work.

Our solution to this quandary is Deserved Run Average (DRA), our core pitching metric. DRA looks like earned run average (ERA), the tried-and-true pitching stat you've seen on every baseball broadcast or box score from the past century, but it's very different. To start, DRA takes an event-by-event look at what the pitchers does, and adjusts the value of that event based on different environmental factors like park, batter, catcher, umpire, base-out situation, run differential, inning, defense, home field advantage, pitcher role and temperature. That mixed model gives us a pitcher's expected contribution, similar to what we do for our DRC+ model for hitters and FRAA model for catchers. (Oh, and we also consider the pitcher's effect on basestealing and on balls getting past the catcher.)

It's important to note that DRA is set to the scale of runs allowed per nine innings (RA9) instead of ERA, which makes DRA's scale slightly higher than ERA's. The reason for this is because ERA tends to overrate three types of pitchers:

1. Pitchers who play in parks where scorers hand out more errors. Official scorers differ significantly in the frequency at which they assign errors to fielders.
2. Ground-ball pitchers, because a substantial proportion of errors occur on groundballs.
3. Pitchers who aren't very good. Better pitchers often allow fewer unearned runs than bad pitchers, because good pitchers tend to find ways to get out of jams.

Seattle Mariners 2020

Since the last time you picked up an edition of this book, we've also made a few minor changes to DRA to make it better. Recent research into "tunneling"—the act of throwing consecutive pitches that appear similar from a batter's point of view until after the swing decision point–data has given us a new contextual factor to account for in DRA: plate distance. This refers to the distance between successive pitches as they approach the plate, and while it has a smaller effect than factors like velocity or whiff rate, it still can help explain pitcher strikeout rate in our model.

New Pitching Metrics for 2020

We're including a few "new" pitching metrics in the book for the 2020 edition, though unlike last year, these numbers may be a little bit more familiar to those of you who have spent some time investigating baseball statistics.

Fastball Percentage

Our fastball percentage (FB%) statistic measures how frequently a pitcher throws a pitch classified as a "fastball," measured as a percentage of overall pitches thrown. We qualify three types of fastballs:

1. The traditional four-seam fastball;
2. The two-seam fastball or sinker;
3. "Hard cutters," which are pitches that have the movement profile of a cut fastball and are used as the pitcher's primary offering or in place of a more traditional fastball.

For example, a pitcher with a FB% of 67 throws any combination of these three pitches about two-thirds of the time.

Whiff Rate

Everybody loves a swing and a miss, and whiff rate (WHF) measures how frequently pitchers induce a swinging strike. To calculate WHF, we add up all the pitches thrown that ended with a swinging strike, then divide that number by a pitcher's total pitches thrown. Most often, high whiff rates correlate with high strikeout rates (and overall effective pitcher performance).

Called Strike Probability

Called Strike Probability (CSP) is a number that represents the likelihood that all of a pitcher's pitches will be called a strike while controlling for location, pitcher and batter handedness, umpire and count. Here's how it works: on each pitch, our model determines how many times (out of 100) that a similar pitch was called for a strike given those factors mentioned above, and when normalized for each batter's strike zone. Then we average the CSP for all pitches thrown by a pitcher in a season, and that gives us the yearly CSP percentage you see in the stats boxes.

As you might imagine, pitchers with a higher CSP are more likely to work in the zone, where pitchers with a lower CSP are likely locating their pitches outside the normal strike zone, for better or for worse.

Projections

Many of you aren't turning to this book just for a look at what a player has done, but for a look at what a player is going to do: the PECOTA projections. PECOTA, initially developed by Nate Silver (who has moved on to greater fame as a political analyst), consists of three parts:

1. Major-league equivalencies, which use minor-league statistics to project how a player will perform in the major leagues;
2. Baseline forecasts, which use weighted averages and regression to the mean to estimate a player's current true talent level; and
3. Aging curves, which uses the career paths of comparable players to estimate how a player's statistics are likely to change over time.

With all those important things covered, let's take a look at what's in the book this year.

Team Prospectus

Most of this book is composed of team chapters, with one for each of the 30 major-league franchises. On the first page of each chapter, you'll see a box that contains some of the key statistics for each team as well as a very inviting stadium diagram. (You can see an example of this for the Milwaukee Brewers on this very page!)

We start with the team name, their unadjusted 2019 win-loss record, and their divisional ranking. Beneath that are a host of other team statistics. **Pythag** presents an adjusted 2019 winning percentage, calculated by taking runs scored per game (**RS/G**) and runs allowed per game (**RA/G**) for the team, and running them through a version of Bill James' Pythagorean formula that was refined and improved by David Smyth and Brandon Heipp. (The formula is called "Pythagenpat," which is equally fun to type and to say.)

Next up is **DRC+**, described earlier, to indicate the overall hitting ability of the team either above or below league-average. Run prevention on the pitching side is covered by **DRA** (also mentioned earlier) and another metric: Fielding Independent Pitching (**FIP**), which calculates another ERA-like statistic based on strikeouts, walks, and home runs recorded. Defensive Efficiency Rating (**DER**) tells us the percentage of balls in play turned into outs for the team, and is a quick fielding shorthand that rounds out run prevention.

After that, we have several measures related to roster composition, as opposed to on-field performance. **B-Age** and **P-Age** tell us the average age of a team's batters and pitchers, respectively. **Salary** is the combined team payroll for all on-field players, and Doug Pappas' Marginal Dollars per Marginal Win (**M$/MW**) tells us how much money a team spent to earn production above replacement level.

Ending this batch of statistics is the number of disabled list days a team had over the season (**IL Days**) and the amount of salary paid to players on the disabled list (**$ on IL**); this final number is expressed as a percentage of total payroll.

Next to each of these stats, we've listed each team's MLB rank in that category from first to 30th. In this, first always indicates a positive outcome and 30th a negative outcome, except in the case of salary—first is highest.

After the franchise statistics, we share a few items about the team's home ballpark. There's the aforementioned diagram of the park's dimensions (including distances to the outfield wall), a graphic showing the height of the wall from the left-field pole to the right-field pole, and a table showing three-year park factors for the stadium. The park factors are displayed as indexes where 100 is average, 110 means that the park inflates the statistic in question by 10 percent, and 90 means that the park deflates the statistic in question by 10 percent.

On the second page of each team chapter, you'll find three graphs. The first is the **2019 Hit List Ranking**. This shows our Hit List Rank for the team on each day of the 2019 season and is intended to give you a picture of the ups and downs of the team's season. Hit List Rank measures overall team performance and drives the Hit List Power Rankings at the baseballprospectus.com website.

The second graph is **Committed Payroll** and helps you see how the team's payroll has compared to the MLB and divisional average payrolls over time. Payroll figures are current as of January 1, 2020; with so many free agents still unsigned as of this writing, the final 2020 figure will likely be significantly different for many teams. (In the meantime, you can always find the most current data at Baseball Prospectus' Cot's Baseball Contracts page.)

The third graph is **Farm System Ranking** and displays how the Baseball Prospectus prospect team has ranked the organization's farm system since 2007.

After the graphs, we have a **Personnel** section that lists many of the important decision-makers and upper-level field and operations staff members for the franchise, as well as any former Baseball Prospectus staff members who are currently part of the organization. (In very rare circumstances, someone might be on both lists!)

www.baseballprospectus.com

Juan Soto LF
Born: 10/25/98   Age: 21   Bats: L   Throws: L
Height: 6'1"   Weight: 185   Origin: International Free Agent, 2015

YEAR	TEAM	LVL	AGE	PA	R	2B	3B	HR	RBI	BB	K	SB	CS	AVG/OBP/SLG
2017	NAT	RK	18	27	3	1	1	0	4	2	1	0	0	.320/.370/.440
2017	HAG	A	18	96	15	5	0	3	14	10	8	1	2	.360/.427/.523
2018	HAG	A	19	74	12	5	3	5	24	14	13	2	0	.373/.486/.814
2018	POT	A+	19	73	17	3	1	7	18	11	8	0	1	.371/.466/.790
2018	HAR	AA	19	35	4	2	0	2	10	4	7	1	0	.323/.400/.581
2018	WAS	MLB	19	494	77	25	1	22	70	79	99	5	2	.292/.406/.517
2019	WAS	MLB	20	659	110	32	5	34	110	108	132	12	1	.282/.401/.548
2020	WAS	MLB	21	630	92	30	3	35	102	85	123	5	2	.284/.382/.543

Comparables: Ronald Acuña Jr., Mike Trout, Tony Conigliaro

YEAR	TEAM	LVL	AGE	PA	DRC+	VORP	BABIP	BRR	FRAA	WARP
2017	NAT	RK	18	27	135	1.5	.333	0.0	RF(9): -1.1	0.0
2017	HAG	A	18	96	181	8.0	.373	1.0	RF(19): -1.9, LF(2): -0.3	0.9
2018	HAG	A	19	74	222	14.5	.405	0.3	RF(14): 1.1, CF(2): 0.2	1.2
2018	POT	A+	19	73	260	15.4	.340	1.4	RF(14): 1.0, LF(1): 0.0	1.6
2018	HAR	AA	19	35	113	3.6	.364	0.0	LF(4): 0.6, RF(4): -0.5	0.1
2018	WAS	MLB	19	494	125	40.5	.338	-0.5	LF(114): 2.7	3.0
2019	WAS	MLB	20	659	136	49.0	.312	1.4	LF(150): -0.8	4.9
2020	WAS	MLB	21	630	133	43.6	.310	-0.1	LF 3	4.8

Position Players

After all that information and a thoughtful bylined essay covering each team, we present our player comments. These are also bylined, but due to frequent franchise shifts during the offseason, our bylines are more a rough guide than a perfect accounting of who wrote what.

Each player is listed with the major-league team that employed him as of early January 2020. If a player changed teams after that point via free agency, trade, or any other method, you'll be able to find them in the chapter for their previous squad.

As an example, take a look at the player comment for Nationals outfielder Juan Soto: the stat block that accompanies his written comment is at the top of this page. First we cover biographical information (age is as of June 30, 2020) before moving onto the stats themselves. Our statistic columns include standard identifying information like **YEAR**, **TEAM**, **LVL** (level of affiliated play) and **AGE** before getting into the numbers. Next, we provide raw, untranslated numbers like you might find on the back of your dad's baseball cards: **PA** (plate appearances), **R** (runs), **2B** (doubles), **3B** (triples), **HR** (home runs), **RBI** (runs batted in), **BB** (walks), **K** (strikeouts), **SB** (stolen bases) and **CS** (caught stealing).

Next, we have unadjusted "slash" statistics: **AVG** (batting average), **OBP** (on-base percentage) and **SLG** (slugging percentage). Following the slash line is **DRC+** (Deserved Runs Created Plus), which we described earlier as total offensive expected contribution compared to the league average.

One of our oldest active metrics, **VORP** (Value Over Replacement Player), considers offensive production, position and plate appearances. In essence, it is the number of runs contributed beyond what a replacement-level player at the same position would contribute if given the same percentage of team plate appearances. VORP does not consider the quality of a player's defense.

BABIP (batting average on balls in play) tells us how often a ball in play fell for a hit, and can help us identify whether a batter may have been lucky or not...but note that high BABIPs also tend to follow the great hitters of our time, as well as speedy singles hitters who put the ball on the ground.

The next item is **BRR** (Baserunning Runs), which covers all of a player's baserunning accomplishments including (but not limited to) swiped bags and failed attempts. Next is **FRAA** (Fielding Runs Above Average), which also includes the number of games previously played at each position noted in parentheses. Multi-position players have only their two most frequent positions listed here, but their total FRAA number reflects all positions played.

Our last column here is **WARP** (Wins Above Replacement Player). WARP estimates the total value of a player, which means for hitters it takes into account hitting runs above average (calculated using the DRC+ model), BRR and FRAA. Then, it makes an adjustment for positions played and gives the player a credit for plate appearances based upon the difference between "replacement level"—which is derived from the quality of players added to a team's roster after the start of the season–and the league average.

The final line just below the stats box is **PECOTA** data, which is discussed further in a following section.

Catchers

Catchers are a special breed, and thus they have earned their own separate box which displays some of the defensive metrics that we've built just for them. As an example, let's check out J.T. Realmuto.

The **YEAR** and **TEAM** columns match what you'd find in the other stat box. **P. COUNT** indicates the number of pitches thrown while the catcher was behind the plate, including swinging strikes, fouls and balls in play. **FRM RUNS** is the total run value the catcher provided (or cost) his team by influencing the umpire to call strikes where other catchers did not. **BLK RUNS** expresses the total run value above or below average for the catcher's ability to prevent wild pitches and passed balls. **THRW RUNS** is calculated using a similar model as the previous two statistics, and it measures a catcher's ability to throw out basestealers but also to dissuade them from testing his arm in the first place. It takes into account factors like the pitcher (including his delivery and pickoff move) and baserunner (who could be as fast as Billy Hamilton or as slow as Yonder Alonso). **TOT RUNS** is the sum of all of the previous three statistics.

Justin Verlander   RHP
Born: 02/20/83   Age: 37   Bats: R   Throws: R
Height: 6'5"   Weight: 225   Origin: Round 1, 2004 Draft (#2 overall)

YEAR	TEAM	LVL	AGE	W	L	SV	G	GS	IP	H	HR	BB/9	K/9	K	GB%	BABIP
2017	DET	MLB	34	10	8	0	28	28	172	153	23	3.5	9.2	176	34%	.283
2017	HOU	MLB	34	5	0	0	5	5	34	17	4	1.3	11.4	43	32%	.194
2018	HOU	MLB	35	16	9	0	34	34	214	156	28	1.6	12.2	290	31%	.272
2019	HOU	MLB	36	21	6	0	34	34	223	137	36	1.7	12.1	300	36%	.219
2020	HOU	MLB	37	15	6	0	29	29	184	138	28	2.3	12.1	248	35%	.274

Comparables: Zack Greinke, A.J. Burnett, Aníbal Sánchez

YEAR	TEAM	LVL	AGE	WHIP	ERA	DRA	WARP	MPH	FB%	WHF	CSP
2017	DET	MLB	34	1.28	3.82	4.03	3.0	97.7	58	11	47.8
2017	HOU	MLB	34	0.65	1.06	3.08	0.9	97.5	59.6	15.1	49.9
2018	HOU	MLB	35	0.90	2.52	2.33	7.3	97.5	61.2	16.2	51.6
2019	HOU	MLB	36	0.80	2.58	2.51	7.9	96.8	49.9	17.5	48.3
2020	HOU	MLB	37	1.01	2.75	2.95	5.3	95.8	54.6	15.1	48.2

Pitchers

Let's give our pitchers a turn, using 2019 AL Cy Young winner Justin Verlander as our example. Take a look at his stat block: the first line and the **YEAR**, **TEAM**, **LVL** and **AGE** columns are the same as in the position player example earlier.

Here too, we have a series of columns that display raw, unadjusted statistics compiled by the pitcher over the course of a season: **W** (wins), **L** (losses), **SV** (saves), **G** (games pitched), **GS** (games started), **IP** (innings pitched), **H** (hits allowed) and **HR** (home runs allowed). Next we have two statistics that are rates: **BB/9** (walks per nine innings) and **K/9** (strikeouts per nine innings), before returning to the unadjusted K (strikeouts).

Next up is **GB%** (ground ball percentage), which is the percentage of all batted balls that were hit on the ground, including both outs and hits. Remember, this is based on observational data and subject to human error, so please approach this with a healthy dose of skepticism.

BABIP (batting average on balls in play) is calculated using the same methodology as it is for position players, but it often tells us more about a pitcher than it does a hitter. With pitchers, a high BABIP is often due to poor defense or bad luck, and can often be an indicator of potential rebound, and a low BABIP may be cause to expect performance regression. (A typical league-average BABIP is close to .290-.300.)

Seattle Mariners 2020

The metrics **WHIP** (walks plus hits per inning pitched) and **ERA** (earned run average) are old standbys: WHIP measures walks and hits allowed on a per-inning basis, while ERA measures earned runs on a nine-inning basis. Neither of these stats are translated or adjusted.

DRA (Deserved Run Average) was described at length earlier, and measures how many runs the pitcher "deserved" to allow per nine innings. Please note that since we lack all the data points that would make for a "real" DRA for minor-league events, the DRA displayed for minor league partial-seasons is based off of different data. (That data is a modified version of our cFIP metric, which you can find more information about on our website.)

Just like with hitters, **WARP** (Wins Above Replacement Player) is a total value metric that puts pitchers of all stripes on the same scale as position players. We use DRA as the primary input for our calculation of WARP. You might notice that relief pitchers (due to their limited innings) may have a lower WARP than you were expecting or than you might see in other WARP-like metrics. WARP does not take leverage into account, just the actions a pitcher performs and the expected value of those actions…which ends up judging high-leverage relief pitchers differently than you might imagine given their prestige and market value.

MPH gives you the pitcher's 95th percentile velocity for the noted season, in order to give you an idea of what the *peak* fastball velocity a pitcher possesses. Since this comes from our pitch-tracking data, it is not publicly available for minor-league pitchers.

Finally, we display the three new pitching metrics we described earlier. **FB%** (fastball percentage) gives you the percentage of fastballs thrown out of all pitches. **WHF** (whiff rate) tells you the percentage of swinging strikes induced out of all pitches. **CSP** (called strike probability) expresses the likelihood of all pitches thrown to result in a called strike, after controlling for factors like handedness, umpire, pitch type, count and location.

PECOTA

All players have PECOTA projections for 2020, as well as a set of other numbers that describe the performance of comparable players according to PECOTA. All projections for 2020 are for the player at the date we went to press in early January and are projected into the league and park context as indicated by the team abbreviation. (Note that players at very low levels of the minors are too unpredictable to assess using these numbers.) All PECOTA projected statistics represent a player's projected major-league performance.

Below the projections are the player's three highest-scoring comparable players as determined by PECOTA. All comparables represent a snapshot of how the listed player was performing at the same age as the current player, so if a

23-year-old pitcher is compared to Bartolo Colón, he's actually being compared to a 23-year-old Colón, not the version that pitched for the Rangers in 2018, nor to Colón's career as a whole.

A few points about pitcher projections. First, we aren't yet projecting peak velocity, so that column will be blank in the PECOTA lines. Second, projecting DRA is trickier than evaluating past performance, because it is unclear how deserving each pitcher will be of his anticipated outcomes. However, we know that another DRA-related statistic–contextual FIP or cFIP–estimates future run scoring very well. So for PECOTA, the projected DRA figures you see are based on the past cFIPs generated by the pitcher and comparable players over time, along with the other factors described above.

Lineouts

In each chapter's Lineouts section, you'll find abbreviated text comments, as well as all the same information you'd find in our full player comments. The only difference is that we limit the stats boxes in this section to only including the 2019 information for each player.

Managers

After all those wonderful team chapters, we've got statistics for each big-league manager, all of whom are organized by alphabetical order. Here you'll find a block including an extraordinary amount of information collected from each manager's entire career. For more information on the acronyms and what they mean, please visit the Glossary at www.baseballprospectus.com.

There is one important metric that we'd like to call attention to, and you'll find it next to each manager's name: **wRM+** (weighted reliever management plus). Developed by Rob Arthur and Rian Watt, wRM+ investigates how good a manager is at using their best relievers during the moments of highest leverage, using both our proprietary DRA metric as well as Leverage Index. wRM+ is scaled to a league average of 100, and a wRM+ of 105 indicates that relievers were used approximately five percent "better" than average. On the other hand, a wRM+ of 95 would tell us the team used its relievers five percent "worse" than the average team.

While wRM+ does not have an extremely strong correlation with a manager, it is statistically significant; this means that a manager is not *entirely* responsible for a team's wRM+, but does have some effect on that number.

PECOTA Leaderboards

If you're familiar with PECOTA, then you'll have noticed that the projection system often appears bullish on players coming off a bad year and bearish on players coming off a good year. (This is because the system weights several previous seasons, not just the most recent one.) In addition, we publish the 50th

Seattle Mariners 2020

percentile projections for each player–which is smack in the middle of the range of projected production–which tends to mean PECOTA stat lines don't often have extreme results like 40 home runs or 250 strikeouts in a given season. In essence, PECOTA doesn't project very many extreme seasons.

At the end of the book, we've ranked the top players at each position based on their PECOTA projections. This might help you visualize just how a given player's projection compares to that of their peers, so that even if a dramatic stat line isn't projected, you can still imagine how they stack up against the rest of the league. ■

Part 1: Team Analysis

Seattle Mariners: Where Are You Going, Where Have You Been?

Jeffrey Paternostro, Jen Mac Ramos and Matthew Trueblood

2019: What Went Right

Uh…March. Bits of April. The Mariners swept their opening two-game set with Oakland in Japan. They were 13-2 on April 11th and led the AL West by four games. They commenced a six-game losing streak the next day and never looked back—or up, depending on your point of view. They went 55-92 the rest of the way. But for roughly two very odd weeks at the start of the season, the Mariners played like a 101-loss team.

There were a few nice surprises, though. Daniel Vogelbach couldn't maintain that 1.600 OPS past the 15-game mark but did finally achieve his Super Saiyan form: Big Beefy Boy Three True Outcomes DH. He also got a child named after him. Kyle Seager missed the beginning months of the season with a hand injury and scuffled at the start, but Corey's older brother rounded into form, slugging .524 in the second half and perhaps allaying fears his 2018 had confirmed a precipitous decline. Tom Murphy was a perfectly fine backup catcher/DH, showing that his plus raw will play outside the friendly environments of the Rockies' system. Liberated from a part-time role with the White Sox, Omar Narváez was good for a 123 DRC+, although defense remained a concept.

In a year where general manager Jerry Dipoto made fewer trades than average—but still a lot of freakin' trades—dealing away Robinson Canó and Edwin Díaz for Justin Dunn and Jarred Kelenic was an early win. Kelenic broke out in the minors after the Mariners made some adjustments to his setup; he now ranks among the ten best prospects in baseball. Dunn repeated Double-A, likely in part to keep him away from the rabbit balls in the PCL, but pitched well enough to earn a September call-up and will have a decent shot at a 2020 Opening Day rotation spot.

Dunn will have that shot in part because the only sure thing in the Mariners' 2020 rotation is Marco Gonzales, who had another perfectly fine third starter-ish season. As for the rest of the arms, you'll find them in the next section.

2019: What Went Wrong

Yusei Kikuchi received the third-largest contract given to any pitcher last offseason and struggled badly his first year stateside. By WARP he ranked as the second-worst pitcher in baseball to the immortal Glenn Sparkman (they finished at -3.64 and -4.19, respectively). By DRA he was the third-worst pitcher behind Sparkman and M's teammate Wade LeBlanc. Major league hitters slugged almost .600 against his fastball, and his peripherals could anonymously slide into the 2019 Orioles rotation with no one the wiser.

Kikuchi arguably wasn't even the worst starting pitcher on the Mariners. LeBlanc had an 8.04 DRA. Félix Hernández's last season in navy and green was an injury-marred disaster, a sad coda to a great career, Hal Ashby's *8 Million Ways to Die*, which coincidentally is what Mariners fans' experienced every time they tuned into a game after Tax Day. The rest of the rotation—minus the 22 very Mike Leake-ish starts from Mike Leake before they traded him—was merely replacement level. The Mariners at times experimented with an opener in front of their soft-tossing lefties, and those pitchers conceded 27 runs in 29 innings. When the bullpen was used more traditionally, the results were only marginally better.

While the offense provided plenty of firepower overall, several of the team's best hitters were shipped out at the deadline for marginal returns despite the team eating most of the remaining money. Elsewhere, Tim Beckham played well for a time, regressed, then was hit with an 80-game PEDs suspension. Mitch Haniger ruptured a testicle. That's a 99th percentile "what went wrong" for any dude. His season was limited to 63 games and the start to his 2020 season was likely to be delayed by late-winter core surgery. Dee Gordon and Mallex Smith were two more examples of the old baseball cliché, "You can't steal first base." Vogelbach finally got a chance and seemed like the Phelps-ian DH he had always hinted at being, but he vanished in the second half (.162/.286/.341). The fast start even kept the Mariners out of the top five of the 2020 draft. —*Jeffrey Paternostro*

Prospect Outlook

You've probably heard the jokes about how the Mariners' system is, well, a joke. Those jokes are wrong. Perhaps it's more accurate to say that they're not entirely right. The M's do have a few guys who are actually good. In the pitching department, there's 2018 first-round pick **Logan Gilbert** casually making his way through the system and piling up strikeouts while doing so. Reliever **Wyatt Mills** struggled in Double-A, which we might expect of a mid-round college sidearmer.

Hitters have more potential. The team's other 2018 first-round pick (via the New York Mets and a trade), **Jarred Kelenic**, has a chance to be a five-tool player. Right now, the biggest question about him is whether his glove plays in center. Catcher **Cal Raleigh** somehow became a dinger machine, hitting 29 between High-A Modesto and Double-A Arkansas. And then there's **Julio Rodriguez**. It's easy to get caught up in the hype about the 19-year-old, but it's not just hype if it's real. A consistent power stroke is his next frontier; he has a quick, compact swing but it's not yet a reliable source of souvenirs. Closest is **Evan White**, a heretofore glove-first first sacker who latterly developed some power. —*Jen Mac Ramos*

2020 Outlook

In every rebuild, there comes a quiet time, and the Mariners experienced theirs over the winter. The heavy lifting of moving contracts and maximizing return on certain trade chips was done in the offseason of 2018-19. Though Haniger, the most valuable remaining trade candidate on the team, had a setback in his recovery from a ruptured testicle, Dipoto still found ways to make trades and keep the wheels of roster change in motion. Each move seemed focused on meeting basic thresholds of quality while preserving opportunities for young players important to the Next Good Mariners Team.

The biggest move in that vein was the one that sent Narváez to Milwaukee. Murphy's strong showing was enough to convince Seattle to commit to him on a short- to medium-term basis, and Narváez's poor pitch-framing made him unhelpful to the rebuilding club. In exchange, Dipoto got a tall A-ball hurler with control issues. More importantly, the Brewers also kicked in their competitive-balance pick in the draft this June. An extra pick (and the extra bonus allowance associated therewith) might help them take the best player available without worrying about the bonus that player will command. Beyond that, it was like a souped-up spud gun: Rapid-fire small potatoes. Carl Edwards Jr., Yoshihisa Hirano, and Kendall Graveman signed cheap big-league deals to deepen the bullpen and rotation. The Mariners also scooped up Astros prospect Yohan Ramírez in the Rule 5 Draft, betting on sky-high strikeout rates in the mid- to upper minors, and claimed Nick Margevicius from the Padres as a backend rotation option.

Brighter days are coming. The surest sign of that, this winter, was the extension to which the team signed White, making it far more likely he'll be the first baseman on Opening Day. White is now under team control for up to nine years and has a chance to become the player fans associate with the turning point—if *this* rebuild pans out. By next winter, there should be a few more players vying for that position too. —*Matthew Trueblood*

Performance Graphs

2019 Hit List Ranking

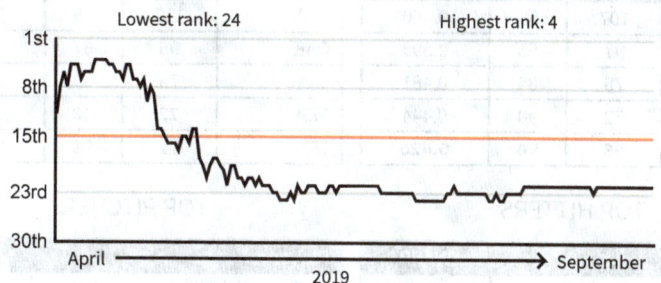

Committed Payroll (in millions)

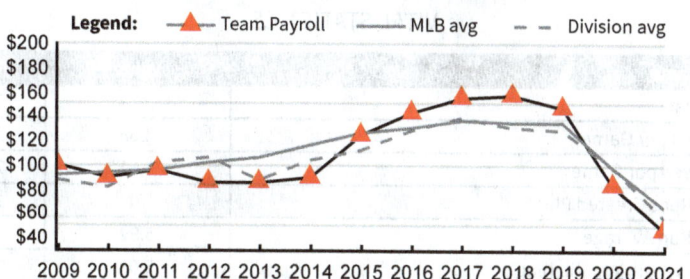

Farm System Ranking

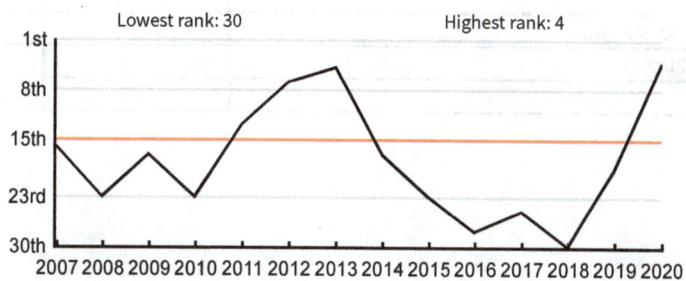

2019 Team Performance

ACTUAL STANDINGS

Team	W	L	Pct
HOU	107	55	0.660
OAK	97	65	0.599
TEX	78	84	0.481
LAA	72	90	0.444
SEA	**68**	**94**	**0.420**

THIRD-ORDER STANDINGS

Team	W	L	Pct
HOU	117	45	0.719
OAK	95	67	0.584
LAA	73	89	0.453
SEA	**72**	**90**	**0.444**
TEX	71	91	0.437

TOP HITTERS

Player	WARP
Omar Narváez	2.3
Kyle Seager	2.2
Tom Murphy	2.0

TOP PITCHERS

Player	WARP
Anthony Bass	1.0
Austin Adams	0.9
Brandon Brennan	0.9

VITAL STATISTICS

Statistic Name	Value	Rank
Pythagenpat	.421	25th
Runs Scored per Game	4.68	20th
Runs Allowed per Game	5.51	26th
Deserved Runs Created Plus	97	15th
Deserved Run Average	5.92	29th
Fielding Independent Pitching	5.03	27th
Defensive Efficiency Rating	.709	10th
Batter Age	27.8	12th
Pitcher Age	29.0	25th
Salary	$146.5M	11th
Marginal $ per Marginal Win	$6.9M	5th
Injured List Days	1188	18th
$ on IL	18%	20th

2020 Team Projections

PROJECTED STANDINGS

Team	W	L	Pct	+/-
HOU	98.3	63.7	0.607	-9
LAA	86.8	75.2	0.536	15
OAK	84.6	77.4	0.522	-12
TEX	73.0	89.0	0.451	-5
SEA	**66.0**	**96.0**	**0.407**	**-2**

TOP PROJECTED HITTERS

Player	WARP
Daniel Vogelbach	2.5
Mitch Haniger	2.5
Tom Murphy	2.0

TOP PROJECTED PITCHERS

Player	WARP
Taijuan Walker	1.0
Carl Edwards Jr.	0.8
Yoshihisa Hirano	0.3

FARM SYSTEM REPORT

Top Prospect	Number of Top 101 Prospects
Jarred Kelenic, #7	4

KEY DEDUCTIONS

Player	WARP
Omar Narváez	0.9
Domingo Santana	0.4
Ryon Healy	0.1
Keon Broxton	0.0
Félix Hernández	0.0
Matt Wisler	0.0
Reggie McClain	-0.2
Anthony Bass	-0.2
Wade LeBlanc	-1.6

KEY ADDITIONS

Player	WARP
Taijuan Walker	1.0
Carl Edwards Jr.	0.8
Evan White	0.7
Yoshihisa Hirano	0.3
Jose Siri	0.1
Brian O'Keefe	0.1
Cody Anderson	0.1
Taylor Williams	0.1
Ljay Newsome	0.0
Yohan Ramirez	0.0

Team Personnel

Executive Vice President and General Manager
Jerry Dipoto

Vice President - Scouting
Tom Allison

Assistant General Manager
Justin Hollander

Assistant General Manager
Joe Bohringer

Manager
Scott Servais

BP Alumni
John Choiniere
Jason Karegeannes

T-Mobile Park Stats

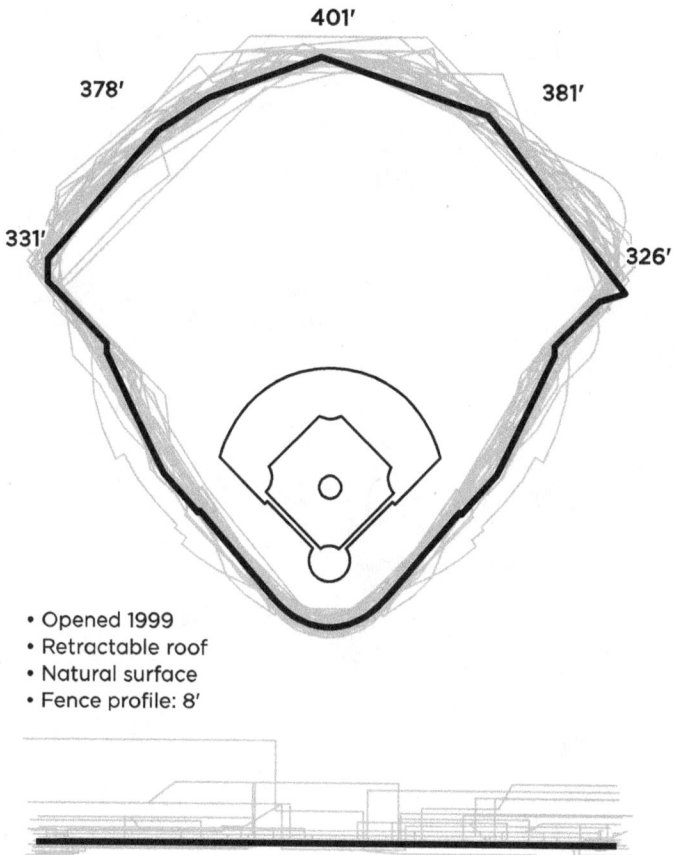

- Opened 1999
- Retractable roof
- Natural surface
- Fence profile: 8'

Three-Year Park Factors

Runs	Runs/RH	Runs/LH	HR/RH	HR/LH
96	97	95	99	95

Mariners Team Analysis

By the time of the Testicle Calamity, any goodwill from the Seattle Mariners' 13-2 start had disappeared. It was June 6th, the fans were thoroughly disengaged, Astros ace Justin Verlander was on the mound, the lineup was being efficiently mowed down, and Mariners were, to nobody's surprise, on the way to their 40th loss of the season.

Mitch Haniger, his teal uniform clashing horribly with T-Mobile Park's neon pink branding, stepped up in the third inning with the Mariners down 3-1. The 2018 All-Star had been expected to push on to new heights, but thanks mostly to a BABIP collapse, Haniger's season had failed to match the team's hopes. And that season was about to get much worse.

Verlander piped in two called strikes to put Haniger in a hole. He missed with the 0-2 pitch, leaving a 94 mph fastball up and in, inducing a defensive swing. Haniger made contact, just about. He quickly wished he hadn't. Rather than dribbling the pitch off to safety, he instead drilled it straight into his own crotch.

Haniger sagged to one knee in pain, touching home plate to steady himself. Somehow, he kept playing for another three innings, toughing his way through a pair of strikeouts before being replaced by Mac Williamson. The wince-inducing news emerged in full the next day: ruptured testicle, season over.

Haniger's loss was metaphor's gain. The Mariners are a self-inflicted ruptured testicle of a team, and four years into general manager Jerry Dipoto's tenure it's difficult to see how they'll contrive to end the longest playoff drought in American sports.

Dipoto's tenure had, until recently, been marked by abortive charges towards the American League Wild Card game. To their credit, the Mariners spent several years resisting the league-wide rebuilding spree, clinging stubbornly to the eroding middle ground and giving themselves a squint-and-*maybe* chance each season. But their repeated almost-contention was fueled by trading every minor leaguer of note for spare parts before the team inevitably fell apart just after each trade deadline, leaving the farm system on life support without anything to show for it at the major-league level.

Three years in, Dipoto changed tack. The core was aging out, and the Wild Card not much of a prize anyway. A rebuild, however, might allow the Mariners to aim at the AL West crown. Granted, that rebuild was rendered more difficult by the fact that Dipoto had spent much of his time at the head of the org merrily torching his own farm system, but it wasn't impossible. In fact, he claimed, it could be achieved in two years. The Mariners would be duking it out with the Astros by 2021:

> "We believe that we have gotten younger, we've gotten more sustainable. And while we wouldn't anticipate that we are a threat to win the World Series in 2019 we do feel like we are better situated to do this come 2020, 2021.

> "We especially use 2021 as a target date just looking at the league around us and how their rosters are built. Looking at the Houston Astros specifically, the Boston Red Sox, Cleveland Indians, we felt that by 2021 either by free agency, age, or looking at their systems, that was the time on the calendar where maybe they would be more susceptible to being caught than they are right now…We view 2021 as that championship-type window if we did this the right way. Building around a group that was from an age perspective in a window that allowed us to crest in 2021."

That 2021 target was the only reason Haniger was on the team in the first place. In a traditional rebuild, he'd have been first out. Trading an All-Star outfielder under team control and heading right into his prime is an excellent way to restock the farm. But Dipoto, hoping that Haniger could anchor the 2021 lineup, kept him while his value was highest. So too Marco Gonzales, whose breakout 2018 would have made him a prime trade target for any team that wanted an upgrade to their starting rotation.

Out of the four club-controlled trade chips Dipoto had to play with: Haniger, Gonzales, James Paxton and Edwin Díaz, only two were dealt. This, naturally, limited Seattle's prospect haul. And the 2021 target influenced Dipoto's decision in other ways. When Robinson Canó (traded), Mike Zunino (traded), Jean Segura (traded), Nelson Cruz (free agent) and a slew of other minor names joined Paxton and Díaz in the Mariners' exodus, the return mostly focused on close-to-the-majors talent capable of plausibly helping the club compete in a short timeframe.

When that sort of player is available on the trade market for a non-stratospheric return, it's because they come with some warts. Take, for instance, Mallex Smith, who can play a premium defensive position and has a terrific batting eye but has serious problems making contact. Or J.P. Crawford, who…can play a premium defensive position (admittedly, better than Smith can) and has a terrific batting eye but has serious problems making contact. Or Domingo Santana, a ferocious hitter who cannot be said to play a defensive position at all. Or Omar Narváez, a wonderful hitter for a catcher but an atrocious receiver.

When the Mariners acquired that quartet, they presumably had plans to tweak their games and spark some sort of breakout. A year into the rebuild, it looks as though those plans have already failed. Crawford and Smith still can't hit, and it turns out Smith can't handle center field either. Narváez still can't catch, although his hitting has improved even further. Santana, meanwhile, had such a difficult time in left field that his tenure in Seattle is already over.

Those four, plus Japanese lefty Yusei Kikuchi, whose introduction to the major leagues fell out of the ugly tree and hit every piece of wood on the way down, constitute the young core meant to supplement the star-level talent in Haniger and Gonzales. Not only has that core failed to gel, but the supposed stars took a significant step back as well. Haniger's season was curtailed early, while Gonzales saw an alarming dip in both fastball velocity and strikeout rate.

So not only was the 2019 edition of the Mariners actively terrible (they ended the season at 64-98, the sixth-worst record in the majors), they displayed exactly none of the development they need in order to hit Dipoto's 2021 contention target. Meanwhile, their biggest obstacle in the AL West handed a debut to 22-year-old DH Yordan Álvarez, who spent four months absolutely torching the American League. The Astros lost Gerrit Cole to free agency, but Álvarez's performance should be a sobering reminder that they're miles ahead of Seattle in both major-league talent *and* player development. Houston's dominance followed a half-decade rebuilding process. The Mariners' attempt to match them on an accelerated schedule is already foundering.

There is, however, some good news. Dipoto's rebuild has managed to erase almost every significant contract from the Mariners' books. Dee Gordon, Kyle Seager and Kikuchi are the only players signed to multi-year deals, and the 2020 season is almost certainly Gordon's last. With so little payroll committed, Seattle is in a position—should they so choose, at any rate—to either go big in free agency themselves or to relieve other teams of problematic contracts in exchange for some prospect help.

Any such help would only make an already flourishing Mariners farm even stronger. Before the 2018 offseason, Dipoto had treated the minor-league system with the sort of cavalier disdain that Haniger apparently has for his own groin. Every ounce of value throughout the organization was squeezed out in exchange for marginal gains in Seattle itself. But now the tide has turned, and not entirely—or even mostly—via trade.

The big name is Jarred Kelenic, of course, who was shipped over from the New York Mets as part of the return for Díaz and Canó. Justin Dunn, Jake Fraley and Justus Sheffield all also arrived through Dipoto's offseason trade extravaganza. But the rest of the major prospects in the new-look Mariners farm are properly home-grown, and almost all took major steps forward last season.

Seattle Mariners 2020

Between Kelenic and 18-year-old wunderkind Julio Rodriguez, it's not impossible that Seattle has the two top outfield prospects in baseball by the end of the 2020 season. Evan White and Kyle Lewis went from best-in-system prospects to top-10s *despite* strong performances in 2019, which can only be a good sign, and both Logan Gilbert and Noelvi Marte had strong professional debuts (admittedly, at very different levels).

Sheffield's struggles aside, 2019 went almost perfectly in the minors, and this is now the sort of farm system that can take a team over the top. Those involved know it, too. When the Washington Nationals battered their way into and through the World Series, it left the Mariners as the only current major-league team to never have won themselves a pennant. That dismal fact spurred Kelenic, Rodriguez and Marte into making a perhaps unwise but nevertheless glorious promise: not for long.

It's easy to look at that promise and the talent piling up in the minor leagues as an indication that better days are ahead. Kelenic and Rodriguez are a prospect pairing worth savoring, one which can support big, even absurd dreams. Right now, however, the Mariners' project looks particularly absurd. The pieces are there on the minor-league level, but for Dipoto's plan to succeed he needs absolutely everything to go right above them.

So far, little has. That's not to say that the situation is irretrievable: one could look at, say, Crawford or Daniel Vogelbach and see a championship-caliber player waiting to be unlocked by making the right tweaks. But even the best player development staff in baseball would need to get very lucky to get the current version of the Mariners firing on all cylinders, and, anyway, results suggest that the Mariners do not have the best player development staff in baseball.

The task would have been much easier had Dipoto given himself more time. Focusing on the current minor-league talent as the giddy culmination of a championship project, rather than merely the opening salvo, has left Seattle building on wobbly foundations. Those foundations could set into something magical, of course, but right now they look like a hope-for-the-best rushed job.

When Kelenic and Rodriguez emerge—*if* they emerge, for we ought to remember that the last time that the Mariners had young players of this caliber around they were called "Dustin Ackley" and "Jesus Montero"—they're capable of catapulting the whole franchise to the next level. But unless Dipoto pulls off some miracles by the end of the 2020 season, the next level for this team looks like a return to soul- (and other-) crushing mediocrity.

—Graham MacAree is an editor at SB Nation.

Part 2: Player Analysis

PLAYER COMMENTS WITH GRAPHS

Tim Beckham SS
Born: 01/27/90   Age: 30   Bats: R   Throws: R
Height: 6'1"   Weight: 205   Origin: Round 1, 2008 Draft (#1 overall)

YEAR	TEAM	LVL	AGE	PA	R	2B	3B	HR	RBI	BB	K	SB	CS	AVG/OBP/SLG
2017	TBA	MLB	27	345	31	5	3	12	36	24	110	5	4	.259/.314/.407
2017	BAL	MLB	27	230	36	13	2	10	26	12	57	1	1	.306/.348/.523
2018	BAL	MLB	28	402	45	17	0	12	35	27	100	1	2	.230/.287/.374
2019	SEA	MLB	29	328	39	21	1	15	47	21	102	1	3	.237/.293/.461
2020	SEA	MLB	30	251	27	11	1	10	31	16	80	2	1	.229/.285/.412

Comparables: Nick Noonan, Robert Andino, Reid Brignac

There was big "Not Mad, Just Disappointed" energy surrounding the news of Beckham's 80-game suspension for the use of performance-enhancing drugs that ended his season in early August. Swaggy T was one of the most popular protagonists in the highly unrealistic April blockbuster, "13-2," punctuating some of its most dramatic scenes with a signature bat flip that even non-Mariners fans grew to recognize. Jerry Dipoto has long preached the value of acquiring former high draft picks, regardless of how sideways their careers may have gone. Had the Mariners struck gold with the former 1.1? Such fantasies were quickly quashed, as Beckham then played a prominent role in another film in the Mariners Cinematic Universe, "37 Errors in 31 Games," as the poster boy for the team's defensive ineptitude. The reality is, No. 1 picks tend to keep getting chances, so don't be surprised if Swaggy T has another supporting role left in the tank.

YEAR	TEAM	LVL	AGE	PA	DRC+	VORP	BABIP	BRR	FRAA	WARP
2017	TBA	MLB	27	345	97	11.0	.357	-0.4	SS(70): -2.2, 2B(17): -0.8	1.0
2017	BAL	MLB	27	230	98	18.8	.376	0.9	SS(49): 3.2	1.4
2018	BAL	MLB	28	402	82	4.8	.282	0.8	SS(49): -3.7, 3B(40): -2.2	0.2
2019	SEA	MLB	29	328	83	4.9	.305	0.9	SS(41): -1.3, LF(13): 1.4	0.6
2020	SEA	MLB	30	251	81	2.6	.305	0.6	SS 0, 3B 0	0.2

Tim Beckham, continued

Batted Ball Distribution

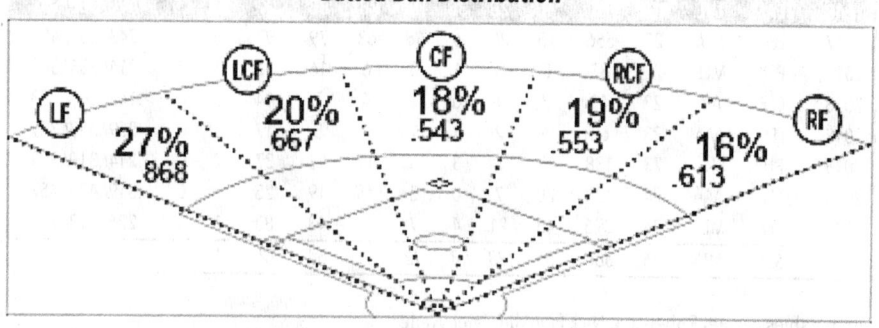

Strike Zone vs LHP   **Strike Zone vs RHP**

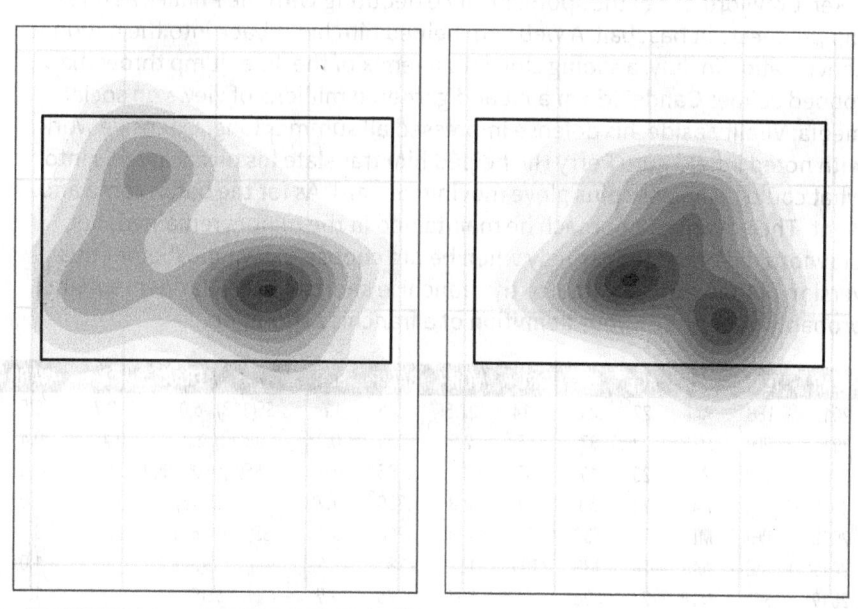

Seattle Mariners 2020

J.P. Crawford SS

Born: 01/11/95   Age: 25   Bats: L   Throws: R
Height: 6'2"   Weight: 180   Origin: Round 1, 2013 Draft (#16 overall)

YEAR	TEAM	LVL	AGE	PA	R	2B	3B	HR	RBI	BB	K	SB	CS	AVG/OBP/SLG
2017	LEH	AAA	22	556	75	20	6	15	63	79	97	5	4	.243/.351/.405
2017	PHI	MLB	22	87	8	4	1	0	6	16	22	1	0	.214/.356/.300
2018	CLR	A+	23	49	8	1	0	1	4	7	14	0	0	.143/.265/.238
2018	LEH	AAA	23	68	6	2	1	1	7	5	17	1	0	.259/.358/.379
2018	PHI	MLB	23	138	17	6	3	3	12	13	37	2	0	.214/.319/.393
2019	TAC	AAA	24	138	20	7	0	3	15	19	25	3	0	.319/.420/.457
2019	SEA	MLB	24	396	43	21	4	7	46	43	83	5	3	.226/.313/.371
2020	SEA	MLB	25	560	55	23	3	12	55	64	121	5	2	.223/.318/.354

Comparables: Daniel Robertson, Nick Franklin, Tyler Wade

A combination of injury, poor performance and lack of opportunity had slowly taken Crawford out of the spotlight since debuting with the Phillies as one of the top prospects in baseball. A web gem helped him burst back into the national conversation in July, a sliding stop into a remix of the Jeter jump throw that robbed Jeimer Candelario of a hit and garnered millions of views on social media. Virality aside, his defense impressed all summer long. Extensive work with noted infield guru Perry Hill helped him translate his physical tools into what could be an easy plus glove moving forward. As for the bat, it came and went. The advanced approach he maintained in the minors remained, but Crawford did damage sparingly when he did choose to swing. Whether this version of Crawford amounts to the franchise shortstop the Mariners sought probably depends on your definition of a franchise shortstop.

YEAR	TEAM	LVL	AGE	PA	DRC+	VORP	BABIP	BRR	FRAA	WARP
2017	LEH	AAA	22	556	114	27.5	.275	1.6	SS(113): -6.0, 3B(6): -0.7	2.5
2017	PHI	MLB	22	87	85	2.9	.306	-0.2	3B(13): 2.3, SS(6): 0.4	0.4
2018	CLR	A+	23	49	47	-1.5	.185	0.0	SS(8): -0.6, 3B(3): 0.5	-0.1
2018	LEH	AAA	23	68	84	2.8	.350	-1.7	SS(16): 0.2	0.0
2018	PHI	MLB	23	138	78	4.8	.286	0.2	SS(30): 0.6, 3B(13): -0.6	0.2
2019	TAC	AAA	24	138	109	16.1	.382	2.6	SS(31): 0.1	1.0
2019	SEA	MLB	24	396	84	10.9	.275	-1.9	SS(93): 4.6	1.3
2020	SEA	MLB	25	560	82	6.8	.273	-1.3	SS 4	1.1

J.P. Crawford, continued

Batted Ball Distribution

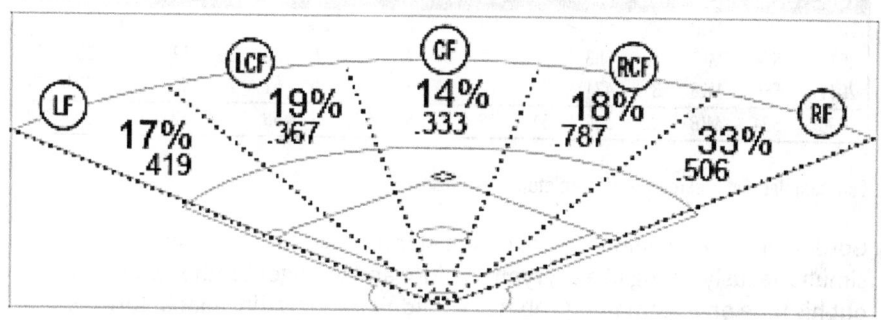

Strike Zone vs LHP   **Strike Zone vs RHP**

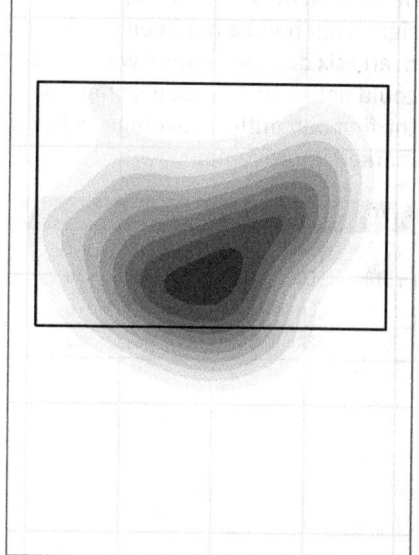

Dee Gordon 2B

Born: 04/22/88 Age: 32 Bats: L Throws: R
Height: 5'11" Weight: 170 Origin: Round 4, 2008 Draft (#127 overall)

YEAR	TEAM	LVL	AGE	PA	R	2B	3B	HR	RBI	BB	K	SB	CS	AVG/OBP/SLG
2017	MIA	MLB	29	695	114	20	9	2	33	25	93	60	16	.308/.341/.375
2018	SEA	MLB	30	588	62	17	8	4	36	9	80	30	12	.268/.288/.349
2019	SEA	MLB	31	421	36	12	6	3	34	18	61	22	5	.275/.304/.359
2020	SEA	MLB	32	560	51	18	5	5	47	23	88	38	12	.272/.306/.353

Comparables: Pat Meares, Garry Templeton, Jack Wilson

Gordon occupies a unique space on the Mariners roster, somehow simultaneously acting like everyone's older and younger brother while playing out his time on a team that probably wouldn't mind trading him before his contract is up. The center field experiment ended with Robinson Canó's departure, leaving Gordon to tend to his traditional second base, where he was far less likely to be GIF'd for everyone's amusement. His biggest offensive development was more than doubling his walk rate from 2018, which would be significant had he not been coming off the lowest single-season walk rate in nearly six decades—there was nowhere to go but up. Not even the juiced ball could help boost Gordon's offensive impact, unless you count skyrocketing from the first percentile in average exit velocity in 2018 to the second in 2019 as a marked improvement.

YEAR	TEAM	LVL	AGE	PA	DRC+	VORP	BABIP	BRR	FRAA	WARP
2017	MIA	MLB	29	695	87	26.4	.354	8.4	2B(153): -0.6, SS(3): 0.0	1.8
2018	SEA	MLB	30	588	76	4.7	.304	4.2	2B(81): 2.5, CF(53): 0.7	0.9
2019	SEA	MLB	31	421	78	2.1	.313	2.2	2B(111): 0.5, SS(2): 0.2	0.5
2020	SEA	MLB	32	560	75	7.7	.318	3.3	2B 2	1.0

Dee Gordon, continued

Batted Ball Distribution

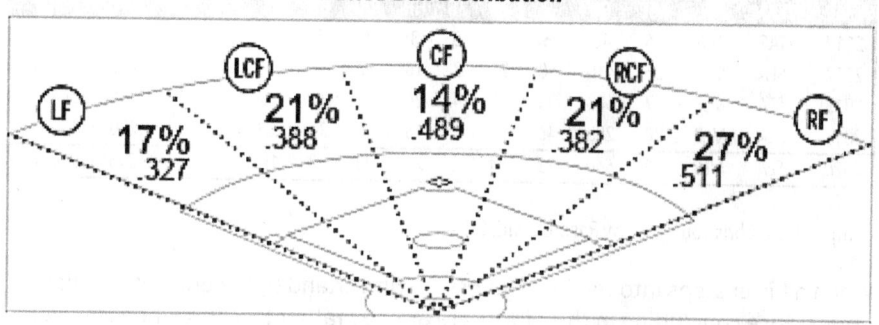

Strike Zone vs LHP   **Strike Zone vs RHP**

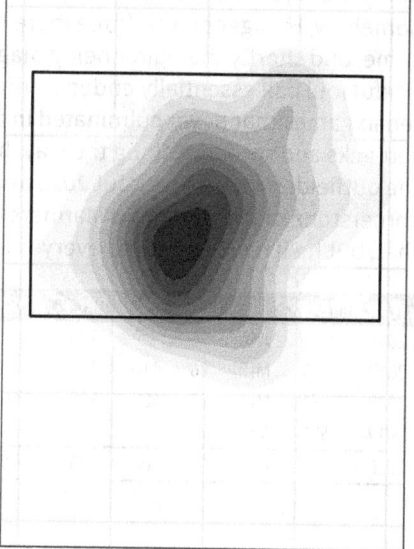

Mitch Haniger OF

Born: 12/23/90 Age: 29 Bats: R Throws: R
Height: 6'2" Weight: 215 Origin: Round 1, 2012 Draft (#38 overall)

YEAR	TEAM	LVL	AGE	PA	R	2B	3B	HR	RBI	BB	K	SB	CS	AVG/OBP/SLG
2017	TAC	AAA	26	48	6	2	0	3	6	7	5	0	0	.256/.375/.538
2017	SEA	MLB	26	410	58	25	2	16	47	31	93	5	4	.282/.352/.491
2018	SEA	MLB	27	683	90	38	4	26	93	70	148	8	2	.285/.366/.493
2019	SEA	MLB	28	283	46	13	1	15	32	30	81	4	0	.220/.314/.463
2020	SEA	MLB	29	560	73	24	2	29	83	53	157	7	3	.246/.330/.477

Comparables: Chris Young, Colby Rasmus, Kirk Gibson

When a hitter steps into the box against Justin Verlander, the odds of the plate appearance concluding in their favor are already rather low. But when Haniger faced off against the future Hall of Famer on June 6th, he would have been overjoyed to have merely escaped with a standard strikeout. Alas, Haniger swung at an inside fastball and fouled it off in the most unfortunate of directions—yeah, there—before flailing at strike three a couple pitches later. Somehow, Haniger played three more innings before being removed from the game, and shortly thereafter being diagnosed with a ruptured testicle. That fateful foul ball essentially ended Haniger's season, save for a few minor-league rehab games that never culminated in a return to the majors, with repeated setbacks and soreness along the way. It was surely a frustrating campaign for the outfielder whose breakout 2018 appeared to situate him as a potential cornerstone of the next good Mariners team. A healthy Haniger may still be just that, but he'll have to remind everyone in 2020.

YEAR	TEAM	LVL	AGE	PA	DRC+	VORP	BABIP	BRR	FRAA	WARP
2017	TAC	AAA	26	48	123	6.5	.219	-1.0	RF(6): 1.4	0.3
2017	SEA	MLB	26	410	115	16.8	.338	-1.4	RF(94): 4.7, CF(6): 0.2	2.0
2018	SEA	MLB	27	683	129	48.6	.336	-3.5	RF(144): 5.0, CF(35): -2.8	3.9
2019	SEA	MLB	28	283	102	8.5	.257	2.0	RF(43): 3.2, CF(24): 0.4	1.4
2020	SEA	MLB	29	560	113	21.8	.300	-1.1	RF 5, CF 0	2.8

Mitch Haniger, continued

Batted Ball Distribution

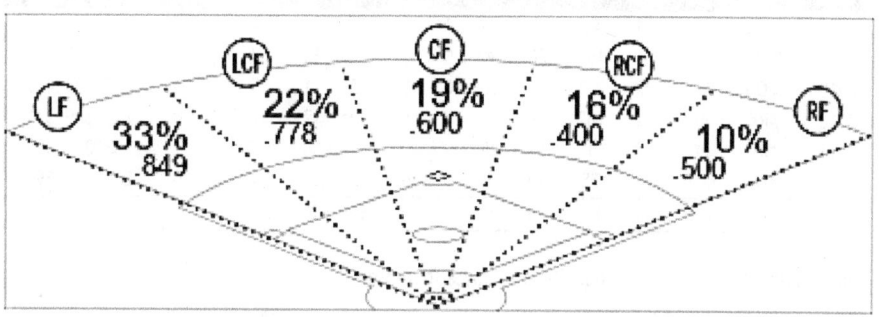

Strike Zone vs LHP   Strike Zone vs RHP

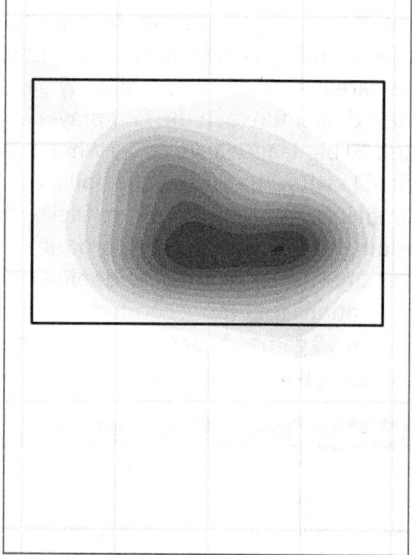

Seattle Mariners 2020

Kyle Lewis   OF
Born: 07/13/95   Age: 24   Bats: R   Throws: R
Height: 6'4"   Weight: 210   Origin: Round 1, 2016 Draft (#11 overall)

YEAR	TEAM	LVL	AGE	PA	R	2B	3B	HR	RBI	BB	K	SB	CS	AVG/OBP/SLG
2017	MRN	RK	21	46	9	2	1	1	7	4	14	1	0	.263/.348/.447
2017	MOD	A+	21	167	20	4	0	6	24	15	38	2	1	.255/.323/.403
2018	MOD	A+	22	211	21	18	0	5	32	11	55	0	0	.260/.303/.429
2018	ARK	AA	22	152	18	8	0	4	20	17	32	1	0	.220/.309/.371
2019	ARK	AA	23	517	61	25	2	11	62	56	152	3	2	.263/.342/.398
2019	SEA	MLB	23	75	10	5	0	6	13	3	29	0	0	.268/.293/.592
2020	SEA	MLB	24	455	48	20	1	17	56	35	159	1	0	.230/.293/.405

Comparables: Zoilo Almonte, Bubba Starling, Trayce Thompson

We were just about ready to close the book on the possibility of "Kyle Lewis, Transcendent Talent." The 2016 Golden Spikes winner who had his game-changing explosiveness sapped by Total Knee Disintegration followed by two rehab-filled and injury-plagued seasons was wrapping up an encouraging, if still unfulfilling, year in Double-A. The offensive tools continued to show up in spurts, and he was finally fully healthy, but the what ifs continued to linger, as if his career were somehow already dead and buried. Then, he became the latest 2019 dinger fun fact: the first player in major-league history to homer in six of his first 10 big-league games. So what in the world happened? Mariners officials cited Lewis as having hit the ball as hard as anyone in their system, but was it as simple as extracting him from Dickey-Stephens Park's bias against righties and adding a livelier baseball to produce these record-breaking results? A sample this small is not worth abandoning several years worth of post-ACL tear evaluations that more comfortably project Lewis as a solid everyday outfielder. But for 10 games in September, you didn't have to squint to see the game-changing player the Mariners fell in love with in 2016.

YEAR	TEAM	LVL	AGE	PA	DRC+	VORP	BABIP	BRR	FRAA	WARP
2017	MRN	RK	21	46	80	4.0	.360	1.4	CF(8): -1.0	0.1
2017	MOD	A+	21	167	110	1.9	.299	-1.5	CF(13): 0.1	0.3
2018	MOD	A+	22	211	104	9.0	.333	0.3	CF(23): -3.1, RF(11): -0.7	0.2
2018	ARK	AA	22	152	91	0.2	.255	-2.0	CF(29): -2.6, RF(1): 0.0	-0.2
2019	ARK	AA	23	517	111	21.4	.367	-3.3	LF(48): 0.1, CF(36): -4.0	0.8
2019	SEA	MLB	23	75	84	0.3	.351	0.8	RF(17): 0.0, CF(2): 0.1	0.1
2020	SEA	MLB	24	455	85	1.2	.327	-0.7	LF -3, RF 0	-0.2

Kyle Lewis, *continued*

Batted Ball Distribution

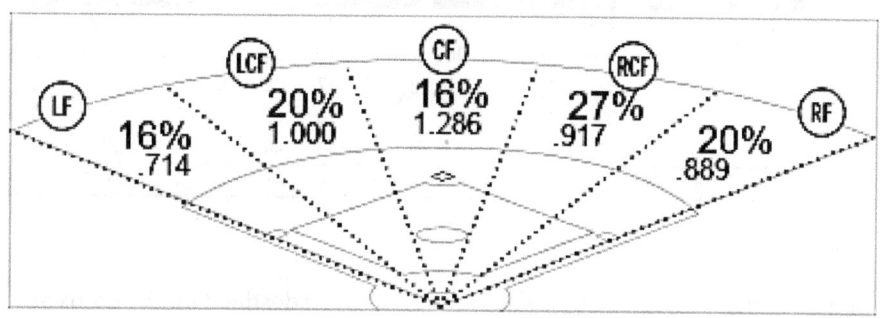

Strike Zone vs LHP **Strike Zone vs RHP**

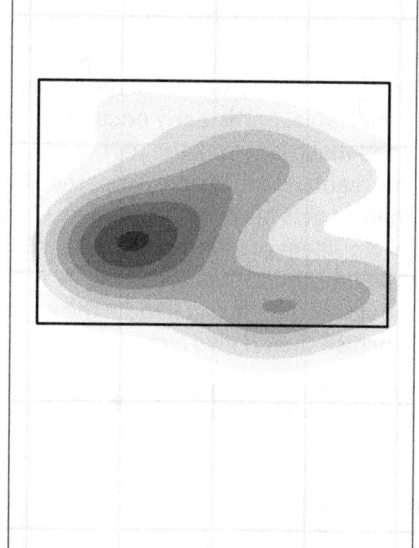

Seattle Mariners 2020

Shed Long 2B

Born: 08/22/95 Age: 24 Bats: L Throws: R
Height: 5'8" Weight: 184 Origin: Round 12, 2013 Draft (#375 overall)

YEAR	TEAM	LVL	AGE	PA	R	2B	3B	HR	RBI	BB	K	SB	CS	AVG/OBP/SLG
2017	DAY	A+	21	279	37	16	1	13	36	27	63	6	3	.312/.380/.543
2017	PEN	AA	21	160	13	6	2	3	14	19	31	3	1	.227/.319/.362
2018	PEN	AA	22	522	75	22	5	12	56	57	123	19	6	.261/.353/.412
2019	TAC	AAA	23	250	38	7	4	9	36	20	65	1	3	.274/.335/.460
2019	SEA	MLB	23	168	21	12	1	5	15	16	40	3	3	.263/.333/.454
2020	SEA	MLB	24	385	41	16	2	13	46	30	104	5	2	.238/.303/.406

Comparables: Jeimer Candelario, Brandon Drury, Brett Phillips

Drafted and developed by Cincinnati, Long appeared destined for the Bronx as the primary return for Sonny Gray before Jerry Dipoto managed to wiggle his way into yet another trade (his 83rd as Mariners GM, to be exact). Whether or not he was invited, he managed to redirect the 5-foot-8 bat-first second baseman towards Seattle in exchange for 2018 second-rounder Josh Stowers. An injury to Dee Gordon rushed Long to the majors after just 32 games in Triple-A, and it showed: His first 19 major-league games featured some spark, but mostly struggle. Upon returning to the big leagues in September, Long looked far more comfortable, particularly once given the keys to the leadoff spot. His size and speed make him look the part of a leadoff hitter, but he sure doesn't swing like one, regularly unleashing what the kids so lovingly refer to as "big daddy hacks" when he gets his pitch. Legitimate thump rests in the bat, although the development of his on-base skills will more likely determine his staying power as an unorthodox leadoff man. Meanwhile, no pressure, but he also has to worry about whether he can handle the keystone; fortunately, the state of the franchise should give him plenty of time to make improvements.

YEAR	TEAM	LVL	AGE	PA	DRC+	VORP	BABIP	BRR	FRAA	WARP
2017	DAY	A+	21	279	156	21.6	.368	-1.1	2B(62): 5.4	2.6
2017	PEN	AA	21	160	102	1.8	.271	-2.4	2B(39): -1.7	0.1
2018	PEN	AA	22	522	114	32.1	.333	3.7	2B(123): -1.9	2.6
2019	TAC	AAA	23	250	75	8.7	.346	0.5	3B(21): -0.9, 2B(21): 0.2	0.2
2019	SEA	MLB	23	168	91	3.2	.327	0.8	2B(24): 1.0, LF(16): -0.4	0.4
2020	SEA	MLB	24	385	88	5.1	.301	0.0	LF -1, 2B 0	0.4

Shed Long, continued

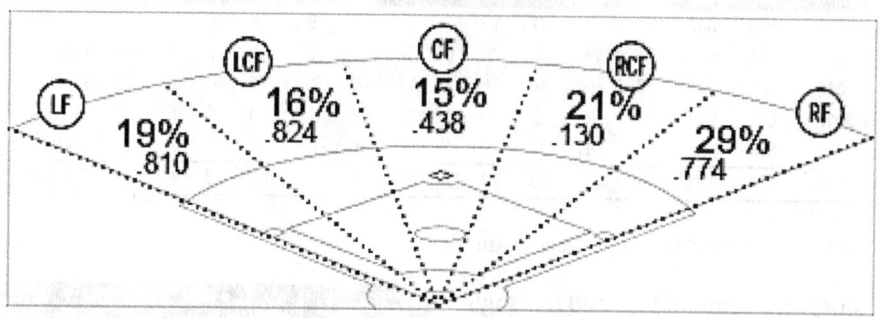

Batted Ball Distribution

Strike Zone vs LHP   **Strike Zone vs RHP**

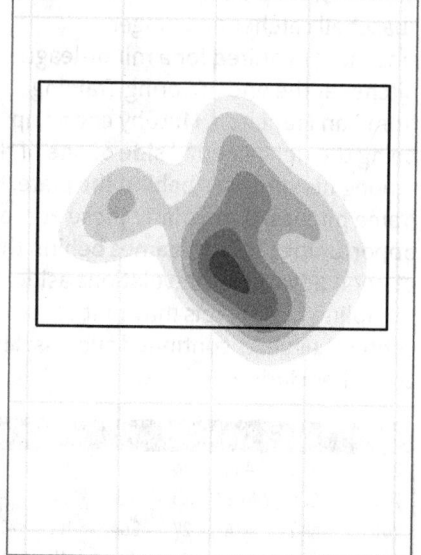

Seattle Mariners 2020

Tom Murphy C
Born: 04/03/91   Age: 29   Bats: R   Throws: R
Height: 6'1"   Weight: 218   Origin: Round 3, 2012 Draft (#105 overall)

YEAR	TEAM	LVL	AGE	PA	R	2B	3B	HR	RBI	BB	K	SB	CS	AVG/OBP/SLG
2017	ABQ	AAA	26	154	22	10	1	4	19	9	56	0	0	.255/.312/.426
2017	COL	MLB	26	26	1	1	0	0	1	2	9	0	0	.042/.115/.083
2018	ABQ	AAA	27	264	40	16	3	17	49	22	76	4	2	.258/.333/.568
2018	COL	MLB	27	96	5	7	1	2	11	3	44	0	1	.226/.250/.387
2019	SEA	MLB	28	281	32	12	1	18	40	19	87	2	0	.273/.324/.535
2020	SEA	MLB	29	455	55	21	2	24	67	30	155	3	1	.238/.295/.466

Comparables: Travis d'Arnaud, Yan Gomes, Stan Lopata

YEAR	TEAM	P. COUNT	FRM RUNS	BLK RUNS	THRW RUNS	TOT RUNS
2017	ABQ	4911	-0.8	0.1	0.4	-0.5
2017	COL	1031	-0.3	0.6	-0.1	0.1
2018	ABQ	7423	3.8	1.0	-0.2	4.6
2018	COL	2791	-0.3	0.0	0.0	-0.3
2019	SEA	9454	3.5	0.8	0.7	4.7
2020	SEA	16624	-1.7	0.4	1.4	0.1

Murphy, a sentient bearded rectangle from upstate New York, gives off strong "hockey defenseman" vibes, a distant cousin of his actual professional sporting occupation of "baseball catcher and dinger smasher." Acquired for a minor-league pitcher at the end of Spring Training from San Francisco, Murphy ended up being the right-handed side of one of the most productive platoons in baseball. Among his surprises behind the plate, Murphy revealed a legitimate ability to frame pitches, particularly those at the lower half of the zone, giving him more opportunities to start games behind the plate, even when he didn't have the platoon advantage. Revelations aside, the bat is his calling card. While the plate discipline peripherals may hint at some incoming regression, his quality of contact suggests continued success: Murphy hit the ball harder on average than any other Mariner in 2019.

YEAR	TEAM	LVL	AGE	PA	DRC+	VORP	BABIP	BRR	FRAA	WARP
2017	ABQ	AAA	26	154	69	1.6	.390	-0.7	C(34): 0.9	0.2
2017	COL	MLB	26	26	54	-2.6	.067	0.2	C(8): 0.5	0.1
2018	ABQ	AAA	27	264	107	18.0	.306	-0.9	C(52): 6.9	2.1
2018	COL	MLB	27	96	45	-2.0	.404	-0.7	C(22): -0.3	-0.3
2019	SEA	MLB	28	281	106	16.4	.340	-0.9	C(67): 4.7, P(3): 0.0	2.0
2020	SEA	MLB	29	455	97	17.3	.315	-0.8	C2	2.0

Tom Murphy, continued

Batted Ball Distribution

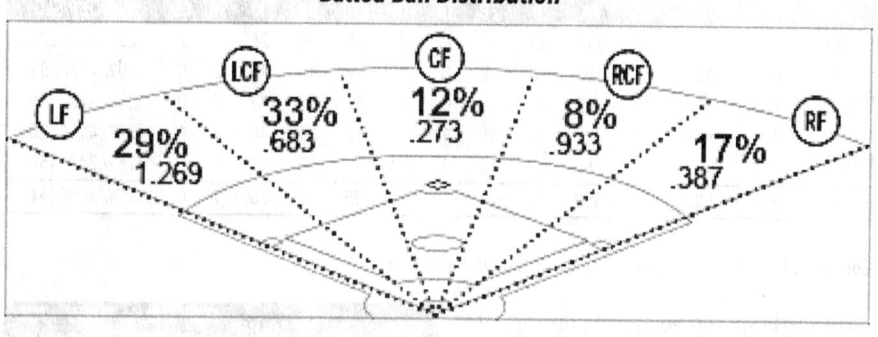

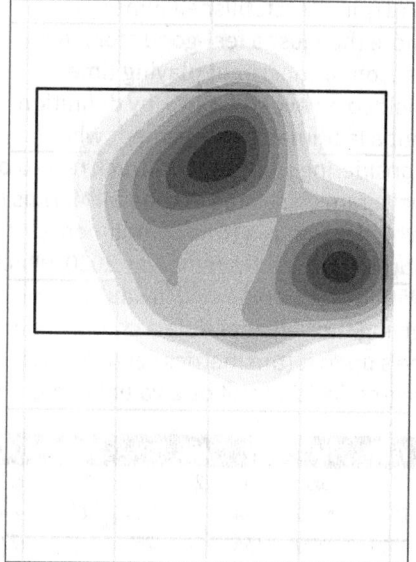

Austin Nola C

Born: 12/28/89 Age: 30 Bats: R Throws: R
Height: 6'0" Weight: 195 Origin: Round 5, 2012 Draft (#167 overall)

YEAR	TEAM	LVL	AGE	PA	R	2B	3B	HR	RBI	BB	K	SB	CS	AVG/OBP/SLG
2017	JAX	AA	27	197	21	7	0	2	25	25	26	3	2	.250/.352/.327
2017	NWO	AAA	27	105	7	4	0	1	6	10	16	0	0	.202/.287/.281
2018	NWO	AAA	28	262	26	16	0	2	32	27	43	2	0	.279/.370/.376
2019	TAC	AAA	29	229	36	15	1	7	37	29	40	4	1	.327/.415/.520
2019	SEA	MLB	29	267	37	12	1	10	31	23	63	1	0	.269/.342/.454
2020	SEA	MLB	30	350	34	13	1	8	35	32	80	1	0	.229/.308/.351

Comparables: Chase d'Arnaud, Paul Janish, Sean Kazmar Jr.

A minor-league free agent signing after seven seasons in the Marlins organization, Nola finally made his big-league debut at age 29 in Seattle, and quickly established himself as more than just a feel-good story. A half season of consistent playing time yielded an average DRC+ by definition, but a legitimate achievement when considering Nola's spotty track record of hitting in the minors. (It also would have ranked second among all Marlins hitters, which, well…you can decide whether that is a Nola compliment or a sick Marlins burn). He'll be a 30-year-old sophomore on Opening Day 2020, which isn't ordinarily a hallmark for success. With Omar Narváez in Milwaukee, however, the organization has discussed giving the versatile Nola a chunk of time behind the plate. If that's the case, and he's up to it (the metrics seem encouraging), he can have that obvious offensive regression and still be a valuable member of the ballclub.

YEAR	TEAM	P. COUNT	FRM RUNS	BLK RUNS	THRW RUNS	TOT RUNS
2017	JAX	5903	0.0	-2.5	0.1	-3.2
2017	NWO	4085	-6.9	-0.9	0.4	-7.7
2018	NWO	9352	3.9	0.0	1.0	4.5
2019	SEA	613	0.1	0.1	0.0	0.3
2019	TAC	4084	2.6	-0.1	0.3	2.8
2020	SEA	7638	1.4	0.4	-0.1	1.7

YEAR	TEAM	LVL	AGE	PA	DRC+	VORP	BABIP	BRR	FRAA	WARP
2017	JAX	AA	27	197	108	6.1	.284	-0.4	C(46): -2.1, 1B(1): -0.1	0.8
2017	NWO	AAA	27	105	65	-2.4	.233	-1.0	C(29): -6.1	-0.6
2018	NWO	AAA	28	262	111	17.0	.333	-2.2	C(68): 6.2	2.1
2019	TAC	AAA	29	229	119	15.7	.377	-3.4	C(28): 2.8, 1B(24): -0.8	1.2
2019	SEA	MLB	29	267	102	6.7	.325	-0.5	1B(59): 2.4, 2B(15): 1.0	0.9
2020	SEA	MLB	30	350	79	2.1	.281	-0.3	C 3, 1B 0	0.5

Austin Nola, continued

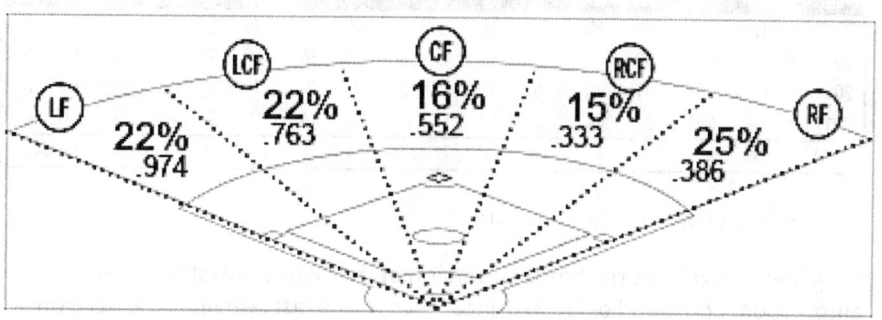

Strike Zone vs LHP   **Strike Zone vs RHP**

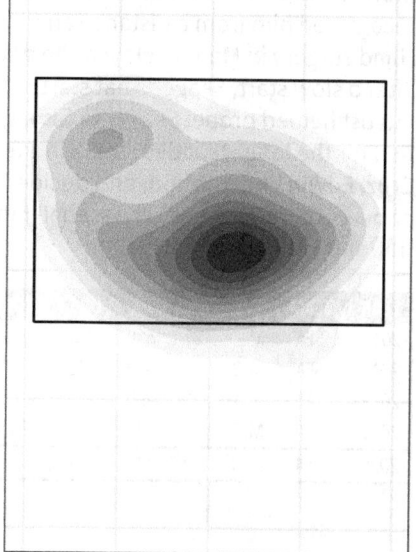

Seattle Mariners 2020

Kyle Seager   3B

Born: 11/03/87   Age: 32   Bats: L   Throws: R
Height: 6'0"   Weight: 210   Origin: Round 3, 2009 Draft (#82 overall)

YEAR	TEAM	LVL	AGE	PA	R	2B	3B	HR	RBI	BB	K	SB	CS	AVG/OBP/SLG
2017	SEA	MLB	29	650	72	33	1	27	88	58	110	2	1	.249/.323/.450
2018	SEA	MLB	30	630	62	36	1	22	78	38	138	2	2	.221/.273/.400
2019	TAC	AAA	31	42	5	2	0	0	7	3	7	0	0	.256/.310/.308
2019	SEA	MLB	31	443	55	19	1	23	63	44	86	2	2	.239/.321/.468
2020	SEA	MLB	32	560	66	27	1	24	75	50	114	3	2	.241/.316/.441

Comparables: Eric Chavez, Ron Santo, Matt Williams

Seager enters 2020 as the baseball version of the "Will Smith standing in an empty room at the end of Fresh Prince" meme, the last remaining player from the 40-man roster GM Jerry Dipoto inherited in September 2015. A relatively dismal 2018 prompted Seager to arrive to Spring Training in, you guessed it, the best shape of his life. Clichés aside, the veteran did report to Peoria leaner and more flexible than ever before, to the point where some teammates hardly recognized him from a distance and his uniforms weren't even fitting quite right. Hand surgery in March delayed the debut of his new physique until May, but after a slow start, Seager's bat started to look more familiar. A scorching hot August helped propel Seager to his eighth (!) consecutive 20-plus homer season, tied for the longest active streak in the majors alongside former Mariners Nelson Cruz, Edwin Encarnación, and decidedly non-former-Mariner Mike Trout. He appears to have staved off baseball hitter mortality for now, but the Grim Reaper (the shift) still looms large.

YEAR	TEAM	LVL	AGE	PA	DRC+	VORP	BABIP	BRR	FRAA	WARP
2017	SEA	MLB	29	650	106	20.6	.262	-5.6	3B(154): 7.4	3.0
2018	SEA	MLB	30	630	90	7.7	.251	-1.6	3B(154): 11.2, 2B(1): 0.0	2.5
2019	TAC	AAA	31	42	71	-2.5	.313	-0.7	3B(5): 0.0	-0.1
2019	SEA	MLB	31	443	113	24.9	.248	-2.4	3B(104): -0.2	2.2
2020	SEA	MLB	32	560	99	10.0	.266	-2.5	3B 5	1.5

Kyle Seager, continued

Batted Ball Distribution

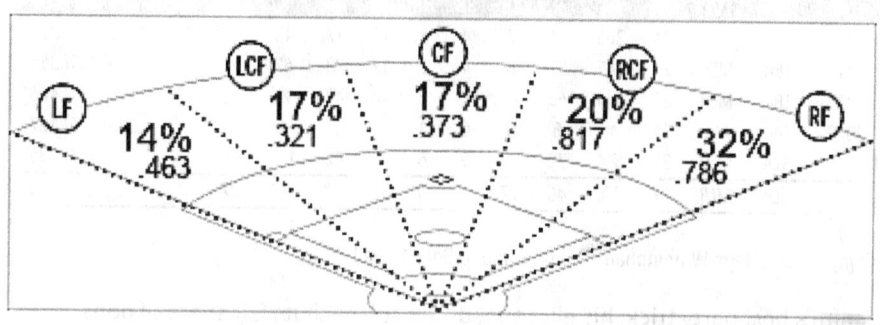

Strike Zone vs LHP

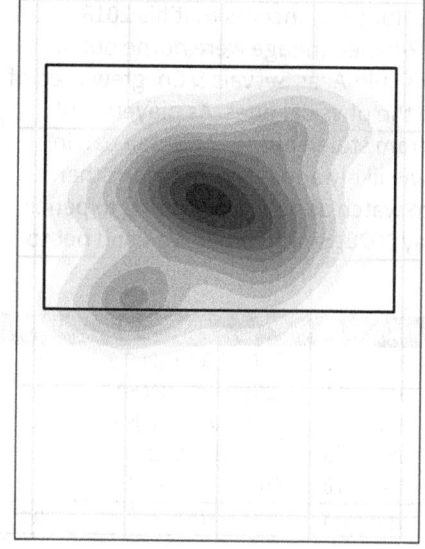

Strike Zone vs RHP

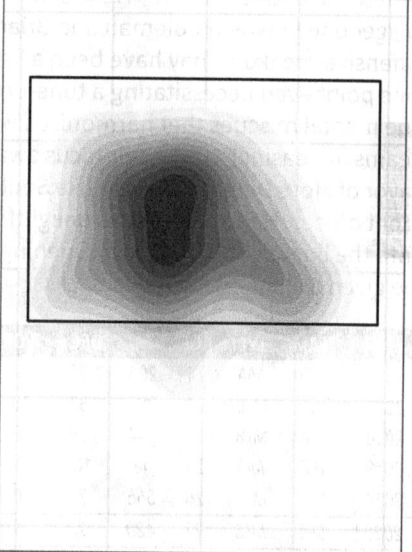

Mallex Smith CF

Born: 05/06/93 Age: 27 Bats: L Throws: R
Height: 5'10" Weight: 180 Origin: Round 5, 2012 Draft (#165 overall)

YEAR	TEAM	LVL	AGE	PA	R	2B	3B	HR	RBI	BB	K	SB	CS	AVG/OBP/SLG
2017	DUR	AAA	24	205	26	7	4	3	10	17	45	21	8	.263/.325/.392
2017	TBA	MLB	24	282	33	8	4	2	12	23	62	16	5	.270/.329/.355
2018	TBA	MLB	25	544	65	27	10	2	40	47	98	40	12	.296/.367/.406
2019	TAC	AAA	26	48	8	3	0	1	6	3	4	7	0	.333/.375/.467
2019	SEA	MLB	26	566	70	19	9	6	37	42	141	46	9	.227/.300/.335
2020	SEA	MLB	27	420	40	17	5	5	36	33	97	27	8	.243/.312/.350

Comparables: Herm Winningham, Dalton Pompey, Boog Powell

Smith's best party trick, his elite speed, can still elicit its fair share of oohs and aahs. He stole a major-league-best 46 bags, including a highly-entertaining "stolen base cycle" on May 28 against Texas. The overall production around his stolen base title, however, did not otherwise reflect a league leader. There's a difference between Rickey Henderson and Vince Coleman, but there's an even bigger one between Coleman and Brian L. Hunter. Concerns that his 2018 offensive breakout may have been a BABIP-fueled mirage were borne out, at one point even necessitating a tune-up in Triple-A, as Servais & Co. grew tired of the mental miscues that harmonized with the physical ones. As players and teams increasingly shift their focus away from stolen bases and small ball in favor of More Dingers, players like Smith will likely appeal more to fans than front offices. He can be just as delightful to watch as he is maddening to pencil into the lineup. Still just 26 on Opening Day 2020, Smith remains a good bet to be given a chance to bounce back.

YEAR	TEAM	LVL	AGE	PA	DRC+	VORP	BABIP	BRR	FRAA	WARP
2017	DUR	AAA	24	205	90	5.1	.333	2.3	CF(33): 5.1, LF(7): 0.5	1.1
2017	TBA	MLB	24	282	83	10.8	.347	2.1	CF(51): -5.2, LF(24): 0.2	0.1
2018	TBA	MLB	25	544	99	28.3	.366	4.4	CF(71): -7.0, RF(47): -1.9	0.9
2019	TAC	AAA	26	48	108	4.5	.350	0.6	CF(10): 0.2	0.3
2019	SEA	MLB	26	566	73	-0.4	.302	6.8	CF(106): -5.9, RF(28): 2.5	0.3
2020	SEA	MLB	27	420	78	6.2	.315	2.5	CF -5	0.1

Mallex Smith, continued

Batted Ball Distribution

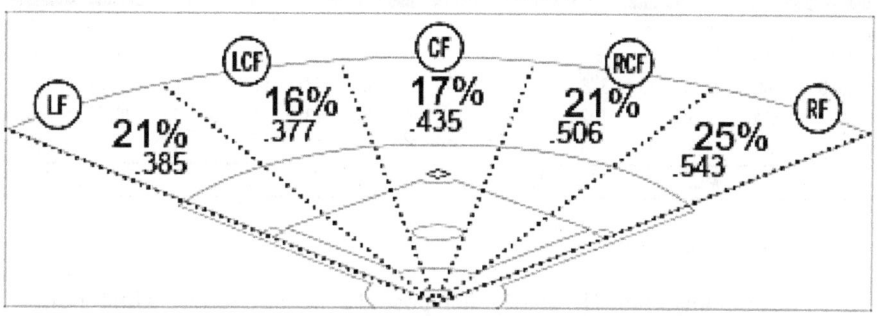

Strike Zone vs LHP   **Strike Zone vs RHP**

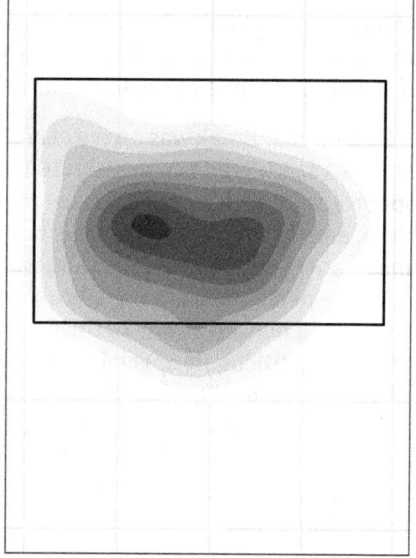

Seattle Mariners 2020

Daniel Vogelbach   DH
Born: 12/17/92   Age: 27   Bats: L   Throws: R
Height: 6'0"   Weight: 250   Origin: Round 2, 2011 Draft (#68 overall)

YEAR	TEAM	LVL	AGE	PA	R	2B	3B	HR	RBI	BB	K	SB	CS	AVG/OBP/SLG
2017	TAC	AAA	24	541	65	25	0	17	83	76	98	3	1	.290/.388/.455
2017	SEA	MLB	24	31	0	1	0	0	2	3	9	0	0	.214/.290/.250
2018	TAC	AAA	25	378	54	16	0	20	60	77	59	0	1	.290/.434/.545
2018	SEA	MLB	25	102	9	2	0	4	13	13	26	0	0	.207/.324/.368
2019	SEA	MLB	26	558	73	17	0	30	76	92	149	0	0	.208/.341/.439
2020	SEA	MLB	27	595	82	22	1	31	88	95	155	1	0	.237/.363/.470

Comparables: Mike Carp, Jeimer Candelario, Justin Smoak

Only Cody Bellinger and Christian Yelich posted a higher OPS in the first month of the season than Vogelbach, who appeared to be loudly answering the question that had followed him for his entire career: 'Will this Chris Farley impersonator actually hit enough to be an everyday designated hitter at the major-league level?' His popularity blossomed further with every home run. It seemed he was the next great chunky cult hero our beautiful game had to offer. Vogey cooled off after April, but his production held steady enough to earn a trip to the All-Star Game as the lone Mariners representative.

Post All-Star Break was an entirely different story. His already-low batting average plummeted to a measly .162 in the second half, severely limiting the opportunities for his prolific power to play. The final picture was that of a good hitter, albeit a rather extreme one: Nearly 49 percent of Vogelbach's plate appearances ended in a home run, walk, or strikeout, the highest Three True Outcome percentage among 135 qualified hitters in baseball. Off the field, he established himself as one of the most likable players in the Seattle clubhouse, creating a particularly special, if unlikely bond with Yusei Kikuchi. How special? Kikuchi's first son, Leo, born in July, was given the middle name "Daniel" in his teammate's honor. Out of options, Vogey's troubling second half may have shortened the leash on his future as the team's designated hitter. However, his beloved organizational presence may give him some breathing room to get his bat back on track.

YEAR	TEAM	LVL	AGE	PA	DRC+	VORP	BABIP	BRR	FRAA	WARP
2017	TAC	AAA	24	541	120	22.5	.332	-7.3	1B(81): -8.3	0.6
2017	SEA	MLB	24	31	82	-3.0	.316	-1.2	1B(7): -0.3	-0.2
2018	TAC	AAA	25	378	161	27.8	.299	-6.0	1B(53): -2.9	2.4
2018	SEA	MLB	25	102	92	0.9	.246	0.6	1B(20): -1.1	0.0
2019	SEA	MLB	26	558	117	21.4	.232	-1.7	1B(57): -3.2	1.6
2020	SEA	MLB	27	595	122	23.9	.280	-1.4	1B -2	2.3

Daniel Vogelbach, continued

Batted Ball Distribution

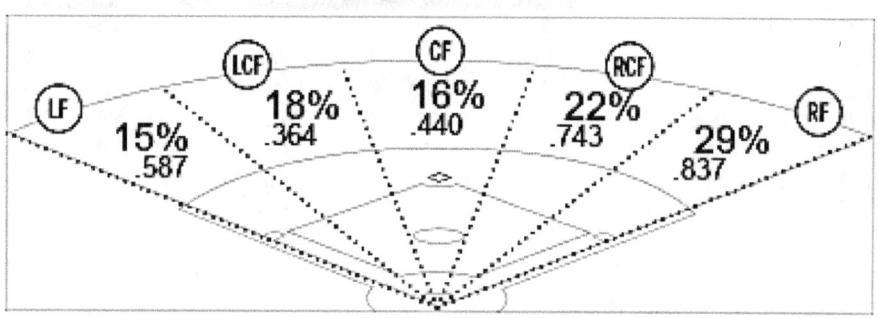

Strike Zone vs LHP   **Strike Zone vs RHP**

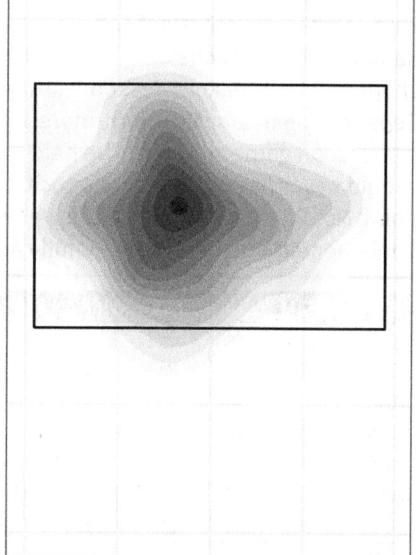

Seattle Mariners 2020

Austin Adams RHP
Born: 05/05/91   Age: 29   Bats: R   Throws: R
Height: 6'3"   Weight: 225   Origin: Round 8, 2012 Draft (#267 overall)

YEAR	TEAM	LVL	AGE	W	L	SV	G	GS	IP	H	HR	BB/9	K/9	K	GB%	BABIP
2017	SYR	AAA	26	6	2	5	44	0	59	44	2	5.6	13.9	91	49%	.321
2017	WAS	MLB	26	0	0	0	6	0	5	4	0	14.4	18.0	10	40%	.400
2018	SYR	AAA	27	1	4	9	41	0	46^1	47	1	3.9	15.2	78	43%	.434
2018	WAS	MLB	27	0	0	0	2	0	1	1	0	27.0	0.0	0	50%	.250
2019	FRE	AAA	28	0	1	1	8	0	10	7	0	2.7	18.0	20	53%	.412
2019	WAS	MLB	28	0	0	0	1	0	1	0	0	18.0	18.0	2	100%	.000
2019	SEA	MLB	28	2	2	0	29	2	31	20	4	4.1	14.8	51	49%	.291
2020	SEA	MLB	29	2	2	4	36	5	38	29	4	4.7	14.4	60	47%	.325

Comparables: Sam Selman, Jeff Stevens, Juan Jaime

Adams showed premium stuff coming up through the minors, but he had never harnessed it as effectively and efficiently as he did in his 31 innings with Seattle following an early-May DFA by the Nationals. Most good relievers have some kind of bizarro aesthetic; Adams pairs his bushy brown beard with an intense habit of vigorously chewing gum while on the mound. Frustratingly, the final chapter of his breakout season featured an ACL tear while covering first base in a September game against Baltimore. Adams' devastating injury in a meaningless late-season game will surely be held up as another example of why pitchers should never have to field their position. How many pitchers must get hurt doing Not Pitching Things before we realize that a designated fielder should be implemented universally? Hopefully Adams is the last.

YEAR	TEAM	LVL	AGE	WHIP	ERA	DRA	WARP	MPH	FB%	WHF	CSP
2017	SYR	AAA	26	1.37	2.14	3.12	1.4				
2017	WAS	MLB	26	2.40	3.60	2.01	0.2	96.5	52.7	14.5	43.7
2018	SYR	AAA	27	1.45	3.50	3.50	0.9				
2018	WAS	MLB	27	4.00	0.00	9.99	-0.1	97.2	58.3	4.2	44
2019	FRE	AAA	28	1.00	2.70	1.64	0.4				
2019	WAS	MLB	28	2.00	9.00	2.35	0.0	95.9	51.5	6.1	35.4
2019	SEA	MLB	28	1.10	3.77	2.65	0.9	97.0	35.2	18.6	45.6
2020	SEA	MLB	29	1.29	3.59	3.62	0.7	96.3	38.9	17	44.3

Austin Adams, continued

Pitch Shape vs LHH

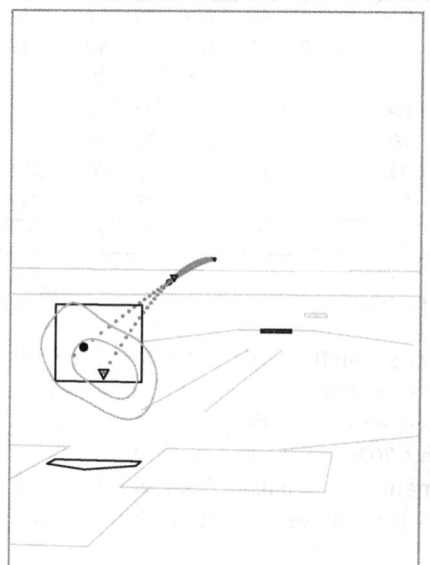

Pitch Shape vs RHH

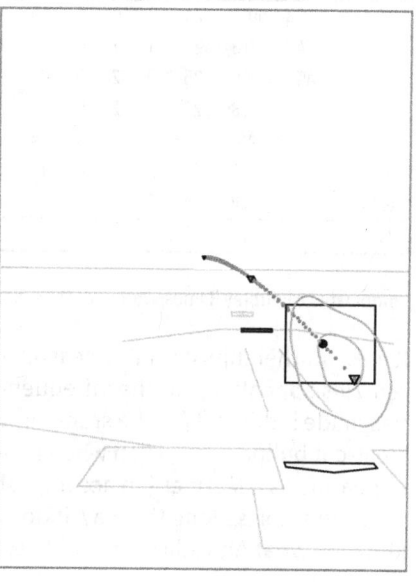

Type	Frequency	Velocity	H Movement	V Movement
● Fastball	33.0%	95.3 [108]	-5.7 [105]	-16.1 [100]
□ Sinker	3.2%	95.7 [116]	-11.7 [106]	-21.8 [95]
+ Cutter				
▲ Changeup				
✕ Splitter				
▽ Slider	63.8%	89.6 [122]	6 [104]	-29.4 [111]
◇ Curveball				
✥ Slow Curveball				
✻ Knuckleball				
▼ Screwball				

Seattle Mariners 2020

Dan Altavilla RHP

Born: 09/08/92   Age: 27   Bats: R   Throws: R
Height: 5'11"   Weight: 200   Origin: Round 5, 2014 Draft (#141 overall)

YEAR	TEAM	LVL	AGE	W	L	SV	G	GS	IP	H	HR	BB/9	K/9	K	GB%	BABIP
2017	TAC	AAA	24	2	0	6	20	0	23^1	17	1	5.8	13.9	36	44%	.340
2017	SEA	MLB	24	1	1	0	41	0	46^2	43	9	3.9	10.0	52	38%	.281
2018	TAC	AAA	25	0	2	0	9	1	6^2	9	2	5.4	9.4	7	35%	.333
2018	SEA	MLB	25	3	2	0	22	0	20^2	11	2	6.5	10.0	23	40%	.209
2019	ARK	AA	26	3	0	4	14	0	16^1	7	1	1.7	13.8	25	42%	.200
2019	TAC	AAA	26	2	1	0	14	0	14	11	0	7.1	16.1	25	48%	.407
2019	SEA	MLB	26	2	1	0	17	0	14^2	9	1	7.4	11.0	18	47%	.242
2020	SEA	MLB	27	2	2	0	31	0	33	26	5	4.7	10.3	37	41%	.272

Comparables: Edubray Ramos, Dominic Leone, Sam Tuivailala

It was another injury-riddled season for the man they call Diesel Dan. The stuff remains appealing, but the infrequency with which it appears in the strike zone has made it difficult for the stunningly swole right-hander to grab hold of a clear-cut bullpen role, even when healthy. 2020 will be his fifth season appearing as a Mariner (an accomplishment in and of itself), but with so many stops and starts along the way, it doesn't feel like we are that much closer to knowing what Altavilla is or could be.

YEAR	TEAM	LVL	AGE	WHIP	ERA	DRA	WARP	MPH	FB%	WHF	CSP
2017	TAC	AAA	24	1.37	1.54	2.74	0.7				
2017	SEA	MLB	24	1.35	4.24	3.88	0.7	99.1	62.4	13.9	48.5
2018	TAC	AAA	25	1.95	9.45	8.16	-0.2				
2018	SEA	MLB	25	1.26	2.61	3.45	0.4	99.0	53.1	13.4	44.3
2019	ARK	AA	26	0.61	1.10	1.81	0.6				
2019	TAC	AAA	26	1.57	8.36	2.80	0.5				
2019	SEA	MLB	26	1.43	5.52	4.53	0.1	98.9	59.3	13.6	46.5
2020	SEA	MLB	27	1.33	3.96	3.97	0.4	98.5	59.7	13.8	46.8

Dan Altavilla, continued

Pitch Shape vs LHH

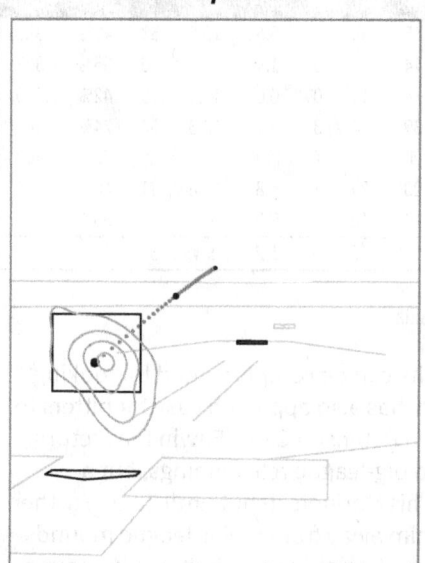

Pitch Shape vs RHH

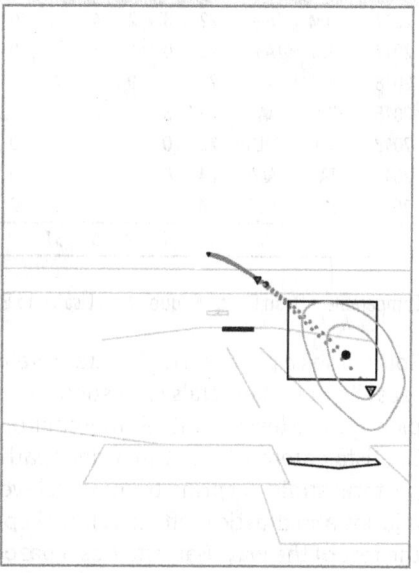

Type	Frequency	Velocity	H Movement	V Movement
● Fastball	59.3%	96.7 [112]	-8 [95]	-11.2 [112]
☐ Sinker				
+ Cutter				
▲ Changeup				
✕ Splitter				
▽ Slider	40.7%	88 [115]	5.9 [104]	-27.4 [117]
◇ Curveball				
✦ Slow Curveball				
✳ Knuckleball				
▼ Screwball				

Seattle Mariners 2020

Gerson Bautista RHP

Born: 05/31/95   Age: 25   Bats: R   Throws: R
Height: 6'3"   Weight: 195   Origin: International Free Agent, 2013

YEAR	TEAM	LVL	AGE	W	L	SV	G	GS	IP	H	HR	BB/9	K/9	K	GB%	BABIP
2017	SLM	A+	22	3	2	4	27	0	45^1	54	2	5.6	10.5	53	41%	.388
2017	SLU	A+	22	0	1	5	10	0	14^1	10	0	1.9	12.6	20	55%	.323
2018	BIN	AA	23	1	0	0	6	0	9^1	12	0	0.0	14.5	15	42%	.500
2018	LVG	AAA	23	3	1	3	31	0	39^2	54	3	4.1	12.3	54	24%	.443
2018	NYN	MLB	23	0	1	0	5	0	4^1	8	2	10.4	6.2	3	35%	.400
2019	TAC	AAA	24	0	0	1	21	0	23^2	29	7	6.8	11.8	31	40%	.361
2019	SEA	MLB	24	0	1	0	8	2	9	13	2	9.0	7.0	7	33%	.355
2020	SEA	MLB	25	1	2	0	31	0	33	37	6	5.2	8.4	31	34%	.317

Comparables: Dean Deetz, Miguel Diaz, Lisalverto Bonilla

Sometimes a pitcher's high-octane velocity can be complimented for looking "easy," but in Bautista's case such velocity has also appeared easy for hitters to pick up. The least-heralded member of the Robinson Canó/Edwin Díaz return, Bautista entered 2019 with a clear path to big-league relief innings, but a pectoral strain in spring training delayed his Mariners debut until June. Further injuries and drastic ineffectiveness kept him away from major-league mounds the rest of the way. Bautista has a bazooka of a right arm, albeit one without a sight, and clearly requires additional refinement before being viewed as a useful bullpen piece. Regardless of his development as a pitcher, he remains an annual top candidate for Time Magazine's Gerson of the Year.

YEAR	TEAM	LVL	AGE	WHIP	ERA	DRA	WARP	MPH	FB%	WHF	CSP
2017	SLM	A+	22	1.81	5.16	6.71	-1.0				
2017	SLU	A+	22	0.91	1.26	2.61	0.4				
2018	BIN	AA	23	1.29	4.82	3.66	0.1				
2018	LVG	AAA	23	1.82	5.22	6.12	-0.4				
2018	NYN	MLB	23	3.00	12.46	7.18	-0.1	100.3	81.1	8.9	52
2019	TAC	AAA	24	1.99	8.75	6.52	-0.1				
2019	SEA	MLB	24	2.44	11.00	6.96	-0.1	99.3	62.9	10.7	44.7
2020	SEA	MLB	25	1.69	6.34	5.91	-0.3	99.3	69.4	10.4	49.1

Gerson Bautista, continued

Pitch Shape vs LHH	Pitch Shape vs RHH
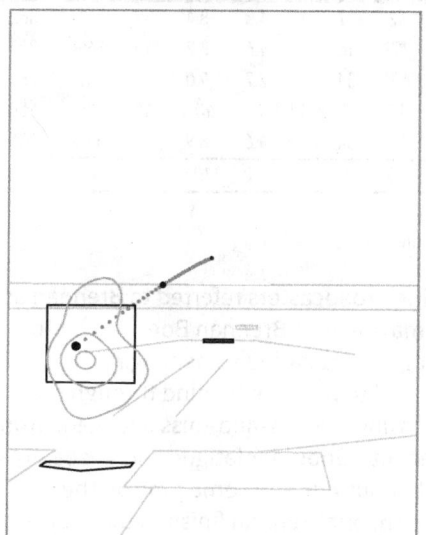	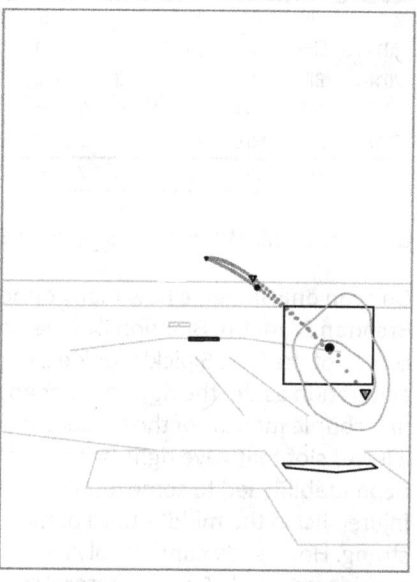

Type	Frequency	Velocity	H Movement	V Movement
● Fastball	62.9%	98 [116]	-2.5 [119]	-9.3 [117]
☐ Sinker				
+ Cutter				
▲ Changeup				
✕ Splitter				
▽ Slider	35.5%	86.4 [108]	4.5 [98]	-32.8 [101]
◇ Curveball				
⊕ Slow Curveball				
✱ Knuckleball				
▼ Screwball				

Brandon Brennan   RHP

Born: 07/26/91   Age: 28   Bats: R   Throws: R
Height: 6'4"   Weight: 220   Origin: Round 4, 2012 Draft (#141 overall)

YEAR	TEAM	LVL	AGE	W	L	SV	G	GS	IP	H	HR	BB/9	K/9	K	GB%	BABIP
2017	BIR	AA	25	2	2	9	28	0	42	47	1	4.3	8.4	39	54%	.362
2017	CHR	AAA	25	0	0	6	14	0	17^2	16	0	4.6	8.2	16	56%	.333
2018	BIR	AA	26	4	3	1	40	1	69^2	54	4	2.7	9.0	70	53%	.266
2019	TAC	AAA	27	1	0	0	9	0	8^2	5	1	4.2	10.4	10	82%	.250
2019	SEA	MLB	27	3	6	0	44	0	47^1	34	6	4.6	8.9	47	54%	.235
2020	SEA	MLB	28	3	2	7	50	0	53	46	6	4.2	10.6	62	54%	.298

Comparables: Kevin McGowan, Curtis Partch, Jed Bradley

One can only imagine how many opposing broadcasters referred to Brennan as Brendan Brannon, Brannon Branden or maybe even Brennan Boesch over the course of the Rule 5 pick's rookie campaign. Devastatingly challenging alliteration aside, the right-hander appeared to be quite the find through the first couple months of the season, showcasing a swing-and-miss changeup from a lower slot that gave right-handed hitters fits. Shoulder fatigue and unseemly dependability led to some less-than-stellar outings and some time on the injured list in the middle-third of the season, but Brennan finished the year strong. He already comfortably cleared the tremendously low bar of what is considered a Rule 5 success story, so any contribution from here on out is gravy.

YEAR	TEAM	LVL	AGE	WHIP	ERA	DRA	WARP	MPH	FB%	WHF	CSP
2017	BIR	AA	25	1.60	5.36	6.14	-0.7				
2017	CHR	AAA	25	1.42	3.06	5.10	0.0				
2018	BIR	AA	26	1.08	3.10	3.32	1.3				
2019	TAC	AAA	27	1.04	1.04	2.69	0.3				
2019	SEA	MLB	27	1.23	4.56	3.60	0.9	96.6	51.6	16.1	43.6
2020	SEA	MLB	28	1.34	3.93	3.98	0.7	96.0	51.9	16.2	43.9

Brandon Brennan, continued

Pitch Shape vs LHH

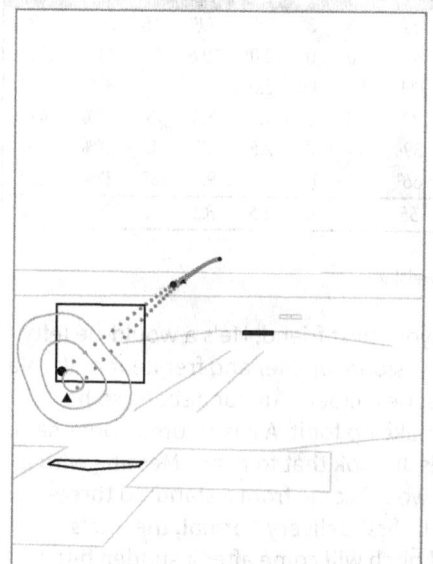

Pitch Shape vs RHH

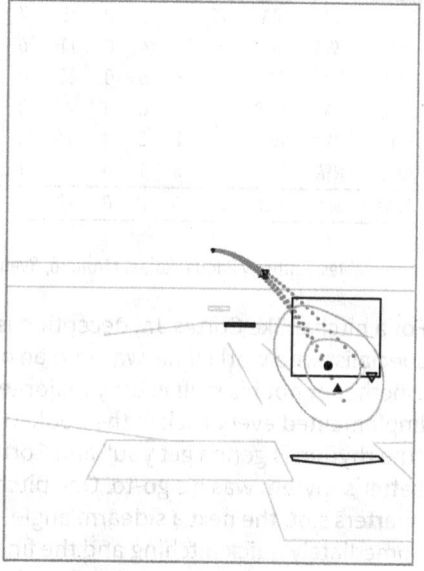

Type	Frequency	Velocity	H Movement	V Movement
● Fastball	51.5%	95.1 [108]	-16.2 [58]	-22.5 [83]
☐ Sinker				
+ Cutter				
▲ Changeup	42.0%	85.1 [99]	-13.9 [87]	-29.2 [95]
✕ Splitter				
▽ Slider	6.5%	87.5 [113]	-0.4 [77]	-28.8 [112]
◇ Curveball				
⊕ Slow Curveball				
✻ Knuckleball				
▼ Screwball				

Seattle Mariners 2020

Nestor Cortes Jr.   LHP
Born: 12/10/94   Age: 25   Bats: R   Throws: L
Height: 5'11"   Weight: 210   Origin: Round 36, 2013 Draft (#1094 overall)

YEAR	TEAM	LVL	AGE	W	L	SV	G	GS	IP	H	HR	BB/9	K/9	K	GB%	BABIP
2017	TRN	AA	22	5	0	0	18	7	52	35	3	3.5	7.8	45	31%	.235
2017	SWB	AAA	22	2	4	0	11	6	48^1	40	0	2.0	10.6	57	41%	.317
2018	SWB	AAA	23	6	6	0	23	18	111^2	95	13	3.0	7.7	96	37%	.261
2018	BAL	MLB	23	0	0	0	4	0	4^2	10	2	7.7	5.8	3	47%	.471
2019	SWB	AAA	24	2	2	0	7	6	39^2	29	3	2.5	9.5	42	38%	.260
2019	NYA	MLB	24	5	1	0	33	1	66^2	75	16	3.8	9.3	69	35%	.321
2020	SEA	MLB	25	3	3	0	42	5	55	57	12	3.5	8.6	52	36%	.297

Comparables: Anthony Banda, Rafael Montero, Ryan Helsley

For a pitcher like Cortes Jr., deception is your best friend. He's a would-be lefty specialist who worked his way into an occasional opener and frequent bulk role. Whether or not his stuff is truly major-league caliber is up for debate, so he implemented every trick in the book to make up for it. A wise woman once said, "the rhythm is gonna get you" and Cortes Jr. took that to heart. Messing with a batter's rhythm was his go-to. One pitch would come from a standard three-quarters slot, the next a sidearm angle. His first delivery normal, then he's immediately quick pitching and the final pitch will come after a sudden hitch that feels minutes long. Replicating his season in Seattle after being traded for international slot money won't be easy with such fringy stuff, but Cortes Jr. isn't much for replication anyways.

YEAR	TEAM	LVL	AGE	WHIP	ERA	DRA	WARP	MPH	FB%	WHF	CSP
2017	TRN	AA	22	1.06	2.60	3.14	1.2				
2017	SWB	AAA	22	1.06	1.49	2.50	1.6				
2018	SWB	AAA	23	1.18	3.71	3.59	2.4				
2018	BAL	MLB	23	3.00	7.71	4.30	0.0	90.9	62	10.2	49
2019	SWB	AAA	24	1.01	3.86	2.61	1.6				
2019	NYA	MLB	24	1.54	5.67	6.48	-0.8	91.8	52.3	11.4	47.9
2020	SEA	MLB	25	1.43	5.27	5.24	0.0	91.5	54.1	11.6	49.6

Nestor Cortes Jr., continued

Pitch Shape vs LHH

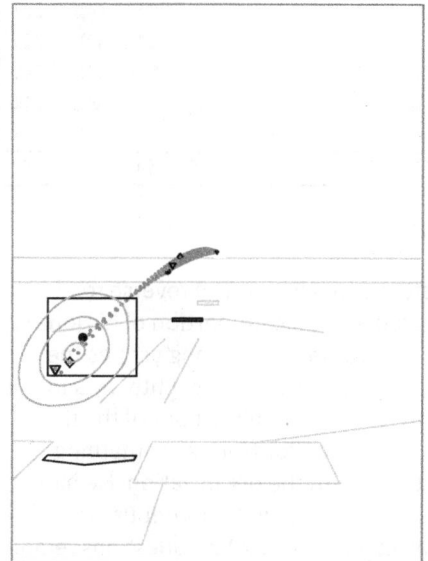

Pitch Shape vs RHH

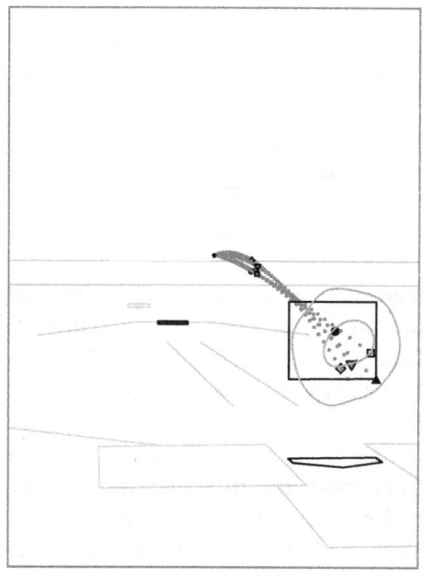

Type	Frequency	Velocity	H Movement	V Movement
● Fastball	47.3%	89.7 [92]	6.1 [103]	-15 [102]
☐ Sinker	4.9%	89 [81]	11.4 [108]	-19 [105]
+ Cutter				
▲ Changeup	12.4%	82.4 [90]	12.6 [93]	-31.9 [87]
✕ Splitter				
▽ Slider	28.4%	82.2 [91]	-4.6 [98]	-32.4 [102]
◇ Curveball	6.9%	76.7 [94]	-5.2 [91]	-41.7 [112]
⊕ Slow Curveball				
✱ Knuckleball				
▼ Screwball				

Justin Dunn   RHP

Born: 09/22/95   Age: 24   Bats: R   Throws: R
Height: 6'2"   Weight: 185   Origin: Round 1, 2016 Draft (#19 overall)

YEAR	TEAM	LVL	AGE	W	L	SV	G	GS	IP	H	HR	BB/9	K/9	K	GB%	BABIP
2017	SLU	A+	21	5	6	0	20	16	95^1	101	5	4.5	7.1	75	44%	.322
2018	SLU	A+	22	2	3	0	9	9	45^2	43	2	3.0	10.1	51	42%	.325
2018	BIN	AA	22	6	5	0	15	15	89^2	85	7	3.7	10.5	105	47%	.345
2019	ARK	AA	23	9	5	0	25	25	131^2	118	13	2.7	10.8	158	38%	.314
2019	SEA	MLB	23	0	0	0	4	4	6^2	2	0	12.1	6.8	5	44%	.125
2020	SEA	MLB	24	6	9	0	23	23	113	121	25	4.5	7.5	94	38%	.288

Comparables: Robert Dugger, Ronald Bolaños, Hunter Wood

Many pitchers make the transition from starter to reliever. The reverse road is one far less-traveled, but Dunn has navigated a significant portion of his journey from skinny college reliever to sturdy big-league starter. A strong year as the horse of the prospect-laden Arkansas squad was soured only slightly by a major-league debut, in which he walked five batters and couldn't get out of the first inning. We'll chalk his dismal debut up to nerves, as control was something Dunn markedly improved upon in his first year with the organization. He hadn't walked more than three in any of the 25 starts leading up to his debut, and slashed his walk rate by a batter per inning compared to 2018. Questions remain about a usable changeup and his ability to brave a lineup three times through, but he's been trending in the right direction on both fronts.

YEAR	TEAM	LVL	AGE	WHIP	ERA	DRA	WARP	MPH	FB%	WHF	CSP
2017	SLU	A+	21	1.56	5.00	6.27	-1.2				
2018	SLU	A+	22	1.27	2.36	3.66	0.9				
2018	BIN	AA	22	1.36	4.22	4.68	0.7				
2019	ARK	AA	23	1.19	3.55	4.61	0.6				
2019	SEA	MLB	23	1.65	2.70	5.32	0.0	94.3	58.8	7.3	42.2
2020	SEA	MLB	24	1.57	6.08	5.80	-0.2	94.1	60.6	7.6	43.5

Justin Dunn, continued

Pitch Shape vs LHH

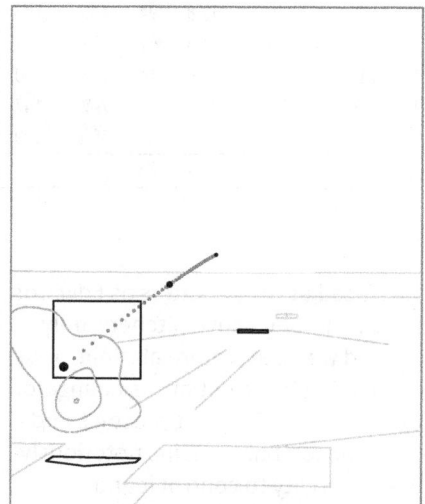

Pitch Shape vs RHH

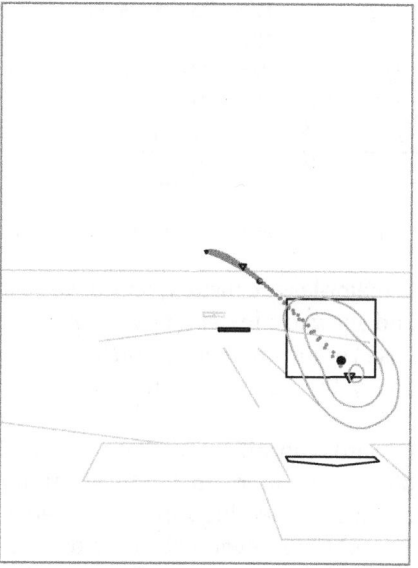

Type	Frequency	Velocity	H Movement	V Movement
● Fastball	58.8%	92.6 [100]	-9.2 [90]	-12.7 [108]
□ Sinker				
+ Cutter				
▲ Changeup	6.6%	87.5 [108]	-13.6 [89]	-22.6 [114]
✕ Splitter				
▽ Slider	34.6%	81.9 [89]	9.7 [120]	-33.7 [98]
◇ Curveball				
✦ Slow Curveball				
✱ Knuckleball				
▼ Screwball				

Seattle Mariners 2020

Carl Edwards Jr. RHP
Born: 09/03/91   Age: 28   Bats: R   Throws: R
Height: 6'3"   Weight: 170   Origin: Round 48, 2011 Draft (#1464 overall)

YEAR	TEAM	LVL	AGE	W	L	SV	G	GS	IP	H	HR	BB/9	K/9	K	GB%	BABIP
2017	CHN	MLB	25	5	4	0	73	0	66^1	29	6	5.2	12.8	94	46%	.193
2018	CHN	MLB	26	3	2	0	58	0	52	36	2	5.5	11.6	67	32%	.281
2019	IOW	AAA	27	2	0	0	14	0	14^2	12	2	3.7	8.6	14	55%	.250
2019	CHN	MLB	27	1	1	0	20	0	15^1	8	3	5.3	10.0	17	24%	.147
2019	SDN	MLB	27	0	0	0	2	0	1^2	4	0	21.6	10.8	2	38%	.500
2020	SEA	MLB	28	3	3	4	56	0	59	44	8	4.7	11.1	73	38%	.262

Comparables: Corey Knebel, Brad Boxberger, Trevor Rosenthal

In major-league history, only Josh Hader has faced as many batters as Edwards and allowed a lower hit percentage. Then again, among active pitchers, only José Leclerc and Kyle Barraclough have allowed walks at a more alarming rate. Lately, the walks have outweighed the outs, leading to demotions, a change-of-scenery trade and his unceremonious release from San Diego at season's end. Edwards can still rack up whiffs, and his high-spin fastball remains notoriously difficult to square up, but he's seemingly lost all ability to control it and continued tinkering with his delivery hasn't helped his results or his headspace. The odds he'll ever reach his closer ceiling are slimmer than Edwards himself, but his still-intact raw stuff makes him a solid fixer-upper opportunity for Seattle.

YEAR	TEAM	LVL	AGE	WHIP	ERA	DRA	WARP	MPH	FB%	WHF	CSP
2017	CHN	MLB	25	1.01	2.98	3.05	1.6	97.1	70	16.1	42.8
2018	CHN	MLB	26	1.31	2.60	4.39	0.3	96.6	75.8	15.6	42.6
2019	IOW	AAA	27	1.23	3.07	3.36	0.4				
2019	CHN	MLB	27	1.11	5.87	5.50	0.0	96.2	76.2	10.2	47.3
2019	SDN	MLB	27	4.80	32.40	3.72	0.0	95.4	66.7	13.7	43.1
2020	SEA	MLB	28	1.27	3.63	3.73	0.9	96.1	73.8	14.9	44.6

Carl Edwards Jr., continued

Pitch Shape vs LHH   **Pitch Shape vs RHH**

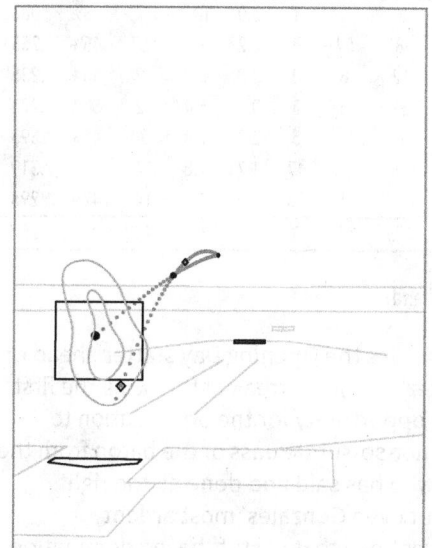 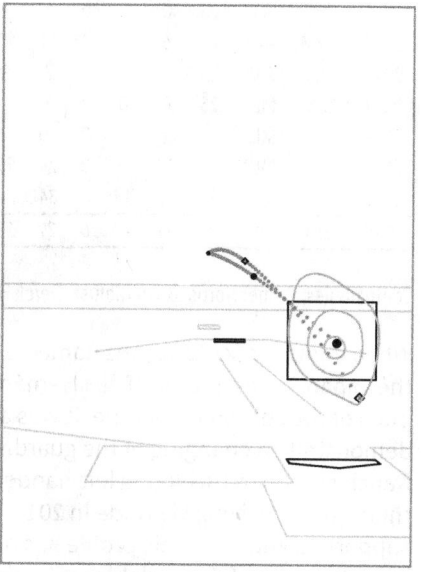

Type	Frequency	Velocity	H Movement	V Movement
● Fastball	74.8%	94.3 [105]	1.4 [137]	-13.3 [107]
☐ Sinker				
+ Cutter				
▲ Changeup				
✕ Splitter				
▽ Slider				
◇ Curveball	22.3%	79.5 [103]	9 [106]	-50.2 [94]
⊕ Slow Curveball				
✱ Knuckleball				
▼ Screwball				

Marco Gonzales LHP

Born: 02/16/92 Age: 28 Bats: L Throws: L
Height: 6'1" Weight: 195 Origin: Round 1, 2013 Draft (#19 overall)

YEAR	TEAM	LVL	AGE	W	L	SV	G	GS	IP	H	HR	BB/9	K/9	K	GB%	BABIP
2017	PMB	A+	25	0	0	0	1	1	6	2	1	0.0	10.5	7	38%	.083
2017	MEM	AAA	25	6	4	0	11	11	68^1	54	6	2.2	7.5	57	45%	.255
2017	TAC	AAA	25	2	0	0	2	2	12	8	0	3.8	6.8	9	56%	.235
2017	SLN	MLB	25	0	0	0	1	1	3^1	6	3	0.0	5.4	2	50%	.273
2017	SEA	MLB	25	1	1	0	10	7	36^2	53	5	2.7	7.4	30	45%	.393
2018	SEA	MLB	26	13	9	0	29	29	166^2	172	17	1.7	7.8	145	45%	.319
2019	SEA	MLB	27	16	13	0	34	34	203	210	23	2.5	6.5	147	42%	.295
2020	SEA	MLB	28	11	11	0	29	29	175	189	30	2.5	6.8	133	42%	.297

Comparables: Daniel Norris, Brian Matusz, Derek Holland

When manager Scott Servais named Gonzales the Opening Day starter ahead of the Japan Series, it broke Félix Hernández's 10-year streak of throwing the first pitch of the season for Seattle. It was an opportunity for the organization to demonstrate a changing of the guard, a not-so-subtle pass of the baton from the franchise icon to the young left-hander who has said and done all the right things since arriving via trade in 2017. But even Gonzales' most ardent supporters know that his profile has never been that of stuff-based domination, but rather one of dependable strike-throwing and consistent competency. In quarterback terms, he's a game-manager. The margin for error is small, however, for pitchers like Gonzales, for whom minor mistakes can snowball into big innings for opponents in a hurry. Staying healthy for another full season was encouraging—there will always be value in showing up for work every day—but chances are he'll start the third game of the year more often than the first from here on out.

YEAR	TEAM	LVL	AGE	WHIP	ERA	DRA	WARP	MPH	FB%	WHF	CSP
2017	PMB	A+	25	0.33	1.50	2.66	0.2				
2017	MEM	AAA	25	1.04	2.90	3.35	1.8				
2017	TAC	AAA	25	1.08	4.50	5.48	0.0				
2017	SLN	MLB	25	1.80	13.50	3.83	0.1	92.7	69	13.8	43
2017	SEA	MLB	25	1.75	5.40	4.51	0.4	93.3	51	9.8	44.5
2018	SEA	MLB	26	1.22	4.00	3.58	3.3	92.2	32.5	10.2	49.4
2019	SEA	MLB	27	1.31	3.99	5.78	0.0	90.3	39.6	8.5	51
2020	SEA	MLB	28	1.36	4.86	4.96	1.2	90.7	38.2	9.3	49.1

Marco Gonzales, continued

Pitch Shape vs LHH

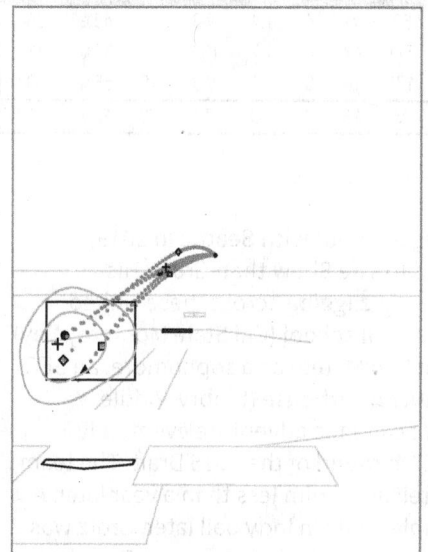

Pitch Shape vs RHH

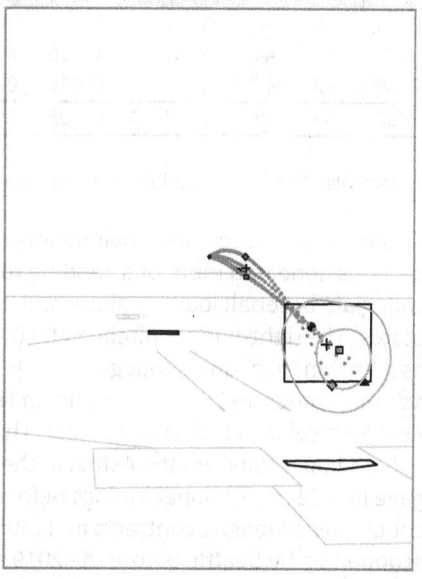

Type	Frequency	Velocity	H Movement	V Movement
● Fastball	18.2%	89.4 [91]	8 [95]	-15.2 [102]
□ Sinker	21.3%	89.3 [83]	12.2 [103]	-18 [108]
+ Cutter	20.5%	85.6 [81]	0.7 [85]	-24.7 [98]
▲ Changeup	24.1%	81.7 [87]	15.3 [81]	-28.6 [97]
✕ Splitter				
▽ Slider				
◇ Curveball	15.9%	76.6 [93]	-6.7 [97]	-52.8 [89]
⊕ Slow Curveball				
✱ Knuckleball				
▼ Screwball				

Mariners Player Analysis - 55

Zac Grotz RHP

Born: 02/17/93 Age: 27 Bats: R Throws: R
Height: 6'2" Weight: 195 Origin: Round 28, 2015 Draft (#829 overall)

YEAR	TEAM	LVL	AGE	W	L	SV	G	GS	IP	H	HR	BB/9	K/9	K	GB%	BABIP
2018	COL	A	25	3	7	0	13	13	80	91	4	1.4	9.3	83	48%	.366
2019	ARK	AA	26	4	4	1	26	6	57^1	47	4	1.7	10.8	69	58%	.312
2019	SEA	MLB	26	1	0	0	14	0	17^1	14	0	4.2	9.3	18	65%	.304
2020	SEA	MLB	27	1	1	0	25	0	26	28	4	3.3	7.6	22	57%	.300

Comparables: Cory Burns, Sam Tuivailala, Josh Roenicke

Of the 21 players to make their major-league debut with Seattle in 2019, perhaps none had more of a winding road to The Show than Grotz. His collegiate baseball journey alone had him zig-zagging across these United States: The right-hander pitched at a Division II school (Cal State Monterey Bay) as a freshman, a junior college (College of San Mateo) as a sophomore, an SEC school (Tennessee) as a junior and an NAIA powerhouse (Embry-Riddle Aeronautical University) as a senior. That academic adventure eventually earned him a call from the Astros in the 28th round of the 2015 Draft. The team gave him 22 professional innings before releasing him less than a year later. A couple minor-league contracts and multiple stints in Indy ball later, Grotz was scooped up by Seattle before the 2019 season and found success in Double-A immediately, prompting a big-league call-up in early August. We could speculate how Grotz fits into the Mariners' bullpen plans going forward, but does it really matter? He's here! He made it!

YEAR	TEAM	LVL	AGE	WHIP	ERA	DRA	WARP	MPH	FB%	WHF	CSP
2018	COL	A	25	1.29	4.61	5.37	-0.2				
2019	ARK	AA	26	1.01	2.51	3.90	0.6				
2019	SEA	MLB	26	1.27	4.15	3.58	0.3	93.7	48.3	8.4	43.1
2020	SEA	MLB	27	1.42	4.96	4.97	0.1	93.2	48.9	8.5	43.6

Zac Grotz, continued

Pitch Shape vs LHH
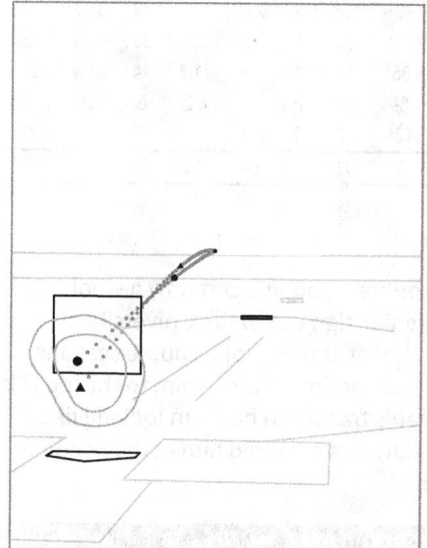

Pitch Shape vs RHH
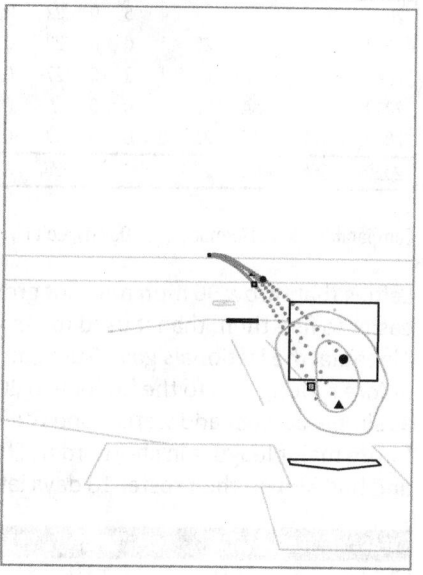

Type	Frequency	Velocity	H Movement	V Movement
● Fastball	36.9%	92.5 [100]	-10 [86]	-16.9 [97]
□ Sinker	11.4%	91.2 [93]	-14.1 [91]	-25.7 [81]
+ Cutter	8.1%	88.1 [96]	0.3 [91]	-26.3 [92]
▲ Changeup	39.6%	82.6 [90]	-6.7 [121]	-38.7 [67]
✕ Splitter				
▽ Slider	4.0%	81.7 [89]	6.9 [108]	-36.6 [90]
◇ Curveball				
✦ Slow Curveball				
✳ Knuckleball				
▼ Screwball				

Mariners Player Analysis - 57

Taylor Guilbeau LHP

Born: 05/12/93 Age: 27 Bats: L Throws: L
Height: 6'4" Weight: 180 Origin: Round 10, 2015 Draft (#314 overall)

YEAR	TEAM	LVL	AGE	W	L	SV	G	GS	IP	H	HR	BB/9	K/9	K	GB%	BABIP
2017	POT	A+	24	4	5	0	23	15	99^1	128	9	2.2	7.1	78	51%	.368
2018	POT	A+	25	1	0	0	28	0	35^2	34	0	3.8	8.8	35	46%	.330
2019	HAR	AA	26	1	2	0	27	0	35	27	1	2.6	11.3	44	61%	.310
2019	FRE	AAA	26	2	0	0	7	0	8^2	10	0	5.2	6.2	6	56%	.370
2019	SEA	MLB	26	0	0	0	17	0	12^1	10	2	2.2	5.1	7	70%	.211
2020	SEA	MLB	27	1	1	0	25	0	26	31	5	3.6	7.3	21	59%	.326

Comparables: Matt Dermody, Kyle Dowdy, Colt Hynes

Lefties that throw 96 mph may not grow on trees, but it's certainly a whole lot easier to find them than it used to be. A senior sign out of the University of Alabama, the Nationals gave Guilbeau a shot at starting for a couple seasons before shifting him to the bullpen in 2018. Sometimes "move him to the 'pen" is as simple as "just add water," and Guilbeau's transition had him looking like a future major leaguer in short order. The Mariners acquired him at the deadline and had him on their roster 18 days later.

YEAR	TEAM	LVL	AGE	WHIP	ERA	DRA	WARP	MPH	FB%	WHF	CSP
2017	POT	A+	24	1.53	5.89	7.00	-2.1				
2018	POT	A+	25	1.37	2.52	4.62	0.1				
2019	HAR	AA	26	1.06	2.31	3.74	0.4				
2019	FRE	AAA	26	1.73	5.19	5.27	0.1				
2019	SEA	MLB	26	1.05	3.65	5.34	0.0	96.2	63.5	8.3	50.2
2020	SEA	MLB	27	1.59	6.05	5.77	-0.2	95.7	64.3	8.4	50.8

Taylor Guilbeau, continued

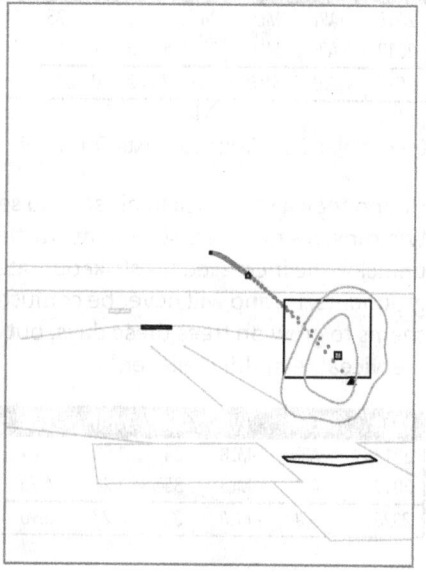

Type	Frequency	Velocity	H Movement	V Movement
● Fastball				
□ Sinker	60.8%	94.7 [111]	13.7 [93]	-21.5 [96]
+ Cutter				
▲ Changeup	29.3%	88 [110]	12.5 [94]	-30.1 [92]
✕ Splitter				
▽ Slider	7.2%	86.5 [109]	0.5 [77]	-32.7 [101]
◇ Curveball				
✥ Slow Curveball				
✳ Knuckleball				
▼ Screwball				

Yoshihisa Hirano RHP

Born: 03/08/84   Age: 36   Bats: R   Throws: R
Height: 6'1"   Weight: 185   Origin: International Free Agent, 2017

YEAR	TEAM	LVL	AGE	W	L	SV	G	GS	IP	H	HR	BB/9	K/9	K	GB%	BABIP
2018	ARI	MLB	34	4	3	3	75	0	66^1	49	6	3.1	8.0	59	51%	.250
2019	ARI	MLB	35	5	5	1	62	0	53	51	7	3.7	10.4	61	46%	.314
2020	ARI	MLB	36	2	2	0	33	0	35	31	5	3.5	9.5	37	48%	.283

Comparables: Jason Motte, Joe Smith, Dan Miceli

Hirano took a step back in his second season. While his ERA rose by more than two runs, his rate stats stayed mostly the same and DRA suggests he was a bit unlucky—he increased his strikeout rate and continued to generate plenty of grounders. Hirano will never be confused for the kind of lights-out reliever who seems to grow on trees these days, but he's pretty much the poster child of "serviceable middle reliever."

YEAR	TEAM	LVL	AGE	WHIP	ERA	DRA	WARP	MPH	FB%	WHF	CSP
2018	ARI	MLB	34	1.09	2.44	4.47	0.3	93.7	53.7	13.5	42.4
2019	ARI	MLB	35	1.38	4.75	4.58	0.4	92.8	47.9	15.1	40.9
2020	ARI	MLB	36	1.27	3.90	4.03	0.5	91.9	49.6	14	40.7

Yoshihisa Hirano, continued

Pitch Shape vs LHH

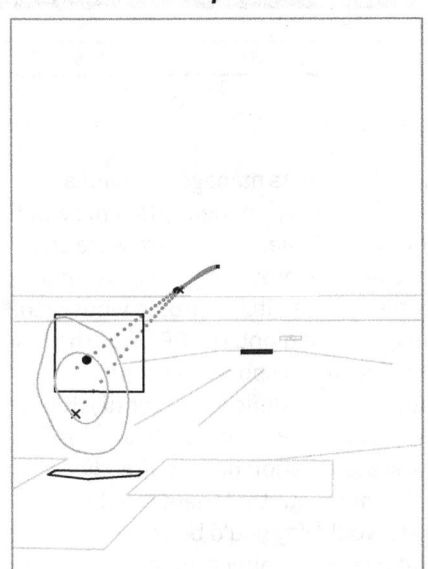

Pitch Shape vs RHH

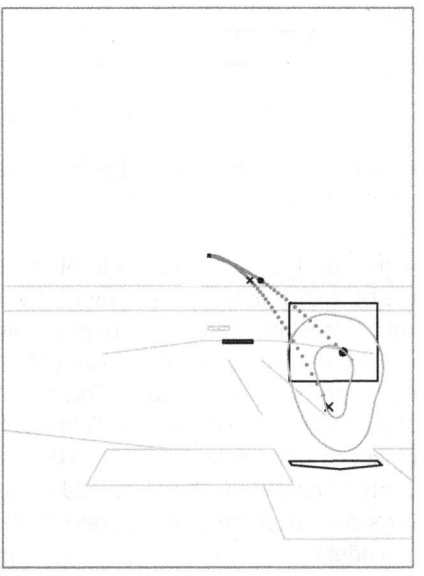

Type	Frequency	Velocity	H Movement	V Movement
● Fastball	47.9%	91.2 [97]	-7.3 [98]	-13.8 [106]
□ Sinker				
+ Cutter				
▲ Changeup				
✕ Splitter	51.7%	84 [95]	-7.8 [100]	-31.9 [91]
▽ Slider				
◇ Curveball				
◈ Slow Curveball				
✳ Knuckleball				
▼ Screwball				

Seattle Mariners 2020

Yusei Kikuchi   LHP
Born: 06/17/91   Age: 29   Bats: L   Throws: L
Height: 6'0"   Weight: 194   Origin: International Free Agent, 2019

YEAR	TEAM	LVL	AGE	W	L	SV	G	GS	IP	H	HR	BB/9	K/9	K	GB%	BABIP
2019	SEA	MLB	28	6	11	0	32	32	161^2	195	36	2.8	6.5	116	45%	.310
2020	SEA	MLB	29	8	10	0	26	26	143	162	28	3.0	6.5	103	44%	.301

Comparables: Ryan Carpenter, Ryan Feierabend, Kei Igawa

A year after missing out on Shohei Ohtani, the Mariners managed to land a different prized Japanese free agent in Kikuchi. Simply not being Japanese Babe Ruth meant that he arrived with considerably less fanfare, but there were still high expectations for a 27-year-old who had already proven himself as one of the best arms in NPB. On its face, this was the type of pitcher profile whose stuff could translate seamlessly. To put it bluntly, it, uh, did not. His DRA was the worst among all qualified starting pitchers. The bright spots, save for an exquisite 96-pitch shutout in Toronto in August, were difficult to identify. Kikuchi also dealt with plenty off the field: his father passed away in March, and his first child was born in July, adding to the cultural assimilation he was already contending with. Optimists could reasonably point out that there are still mid-rotation starter ingredients present. Realists would say you'd be stretching to consider Kikuchi's rookie year anything but a rank disappointment.

YEAR	TEAM	LVL	AGE	WHIP	ERA	DRA	WARP	MPH	FB%	WHF	CSP
2019	SEA	MLB	28	1.52	5.46	7.85	-3.6	95.5	49.1	9.5	50.8
2020	SEA	MLB	29	1.48	5.63	5.55	0.1	94.8	49.1	9.5	50.8

Yusei Kikuchi, continued

Pitch Shape vs LHH

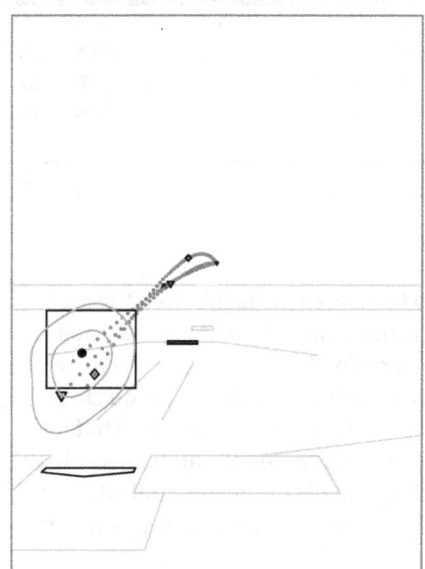

Pitch Shape vs RHH

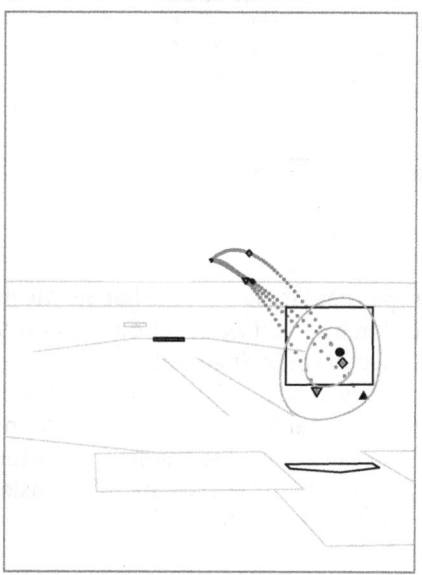

Type	Frequency	Velocity	H Movement	V Movement
● Fastball	49.1%	92.9 [101]	5.3 [107]	-14.6 [104]
☐ Sinker				
+ Cutter				
▲ Changeup	7.5%	84.8 [98]	10.6 [103]	-26.3 [103]
✕ Splitter				
▽ Slider	28.0%	86.3 [108]	-2.8 [91]	-30.1 [109]
◇ Curveball	15.4%	75.5 [90]	-5.6 [92]	-56.1 [82]
⬥ Slow Curveball				
✱ Knuckleball				
▼ Screwball				

Seattle Mariners 2020

Matt Magill RHP
Born: 11/10/89 Age: 30 Bats: R Throws: R
Height: 6'3" Weight: 210 Origin: Round 31, 2008 Draft (#937 overall)

YEAR	TEAM	LVL	AGE	W	L	SV	G	GS	IP	H	HR	BB/9	K/9	K	GB%	BABIP
2017	ELP	AAA	27	6	5	0	19	17	95^2	105	13	3.9	6.9	73	45%	.316
2018	ROC	AAA	28	0	0	2	5	0	8^2	5	0	2.1	13.5	13	28%	.278
2018	MIN	MLB	28	3	3	0	40	0	56^2	58	11	3.7	8.9	56	35%	.301
2019	SEA	MLB	29	3	2	5	22	0	22^1	21	3	2.0	11.3	28	43%	.300
2019	MIN	MLB	29	2	0	0	28	0	28^1	30	4	4.8	11.4	36	36%	.342
2020	SEA	MLB	30	3	3	14	56	0	59	54	8	3.8	10.3	67	40%	.302

Comparables: Michael Blazek, Allen Webster, Steve Johnson

It was hard to parse just what Seattle may have seen in Magill when they claimed him off waivers from Minnesota, other than a desire to add to their collection of Bullpen Matts. But the hard-throwing Magill halved his walk rate immediately upon arrival, a shocking development considering his decade-long professional track record. His newfound control and above-average whiff rate even earned him the few save opportunities of his career. It's quite possible this stretch with the M's was merely a misleading blip of competent control and he'll revert to his traditional wildness in due time. For now, he looks like he might belong.

YEAR	TEAM	LVL	AGE	WHIP	ERA	DRA	WARP	MPH	FB%	WHF	CSP
2017	ELP	AAA	27	1.53	3.95	4.66	1.1				
2018	ROC	AAA	28	0.81	0.00	2.68	0.2				
2018	MIN	MLB	28	1.43	3.81	5.42	-0.3	96.7	60.9	11.8	46
2019	SEA	MLB	29	1.16	3.63	3.18	0.5	96.7	56.9	16.8	45.4
2019	MIN	MLB	29	1.59	4.45	6.11	-0.2	97.5	47.2	14.6	45.4
2020	SEA	MLB	30	1.34	4.26	4.34	0.5	96.2	55.7	13.7	45.5

Matt Magill, continued

Pitch Shape vs LHH

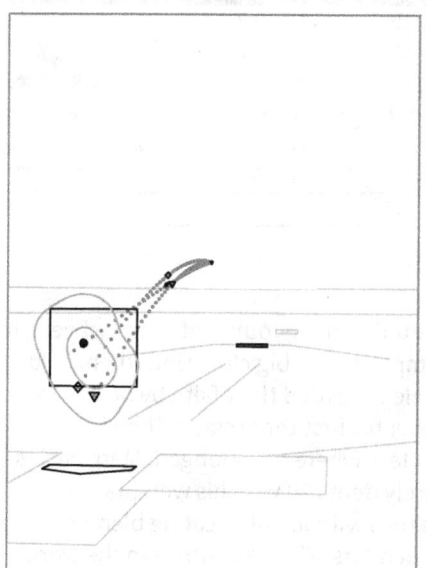

Pitch Shape vs RHH

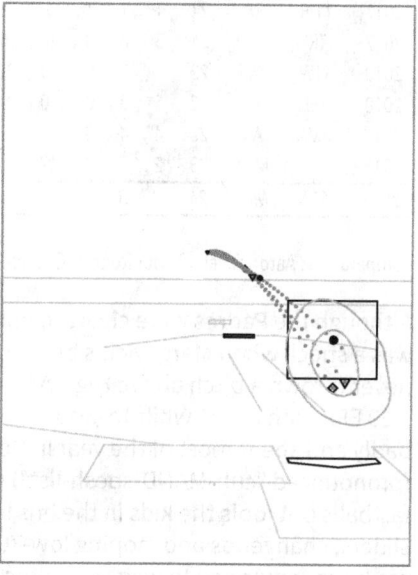

Type	Frequency	Velocity	H Movement	V Movement
● Fastball	51.2%	95.7 [109]	-6.6 [101]	-11.8 [111]
□ Sinker				
+ Cutter				
▲ Changeup				
✕ Splitter				
▽ Slider	26.8%	88.3 [117]	3.7 [95]	-31.2 [105]
◇ Curveball	22.0%	86.1 [125]	3.6 [84]	-39.4 [117]
⬥ Slow Curveball				
✳ Knuckleball				
▼ Screwball				

Nick Margevicius   LHP

Born: 06/18/96 Age: 24 Bats: L Throws: L
Height: 6'5" Weight: 220 Origin: Round 7, 2017 Draft (#198 overall)

YEAR	TEAM	LVL	AGE	W	L	SV	G	GS	IP	H	HR	BB/9	K/9	K	GB%	BABIP
2017	PDR	RK	21	1	1	1	5	4	19	19	0	1.9	14.2	30	61%	.413
2017	TRI	A-	21	3	0	0	6	6	29	20	1	1.2	9.9	32	49%	.260
2018	FTW	A	22	5	5	0	13	13	76^1	79	5	1.1	10.3	87	40%	.346
2018	LEL	A+	22	5	3	0	10	9	58^2	69	5	1.2	9.1	59	39%	.376
2019	AMA	AA	23	4	4	0	12	12	69	75	14	1.7	6.9	53	44%	.296
2019	SDN	MLB	23	2	6	0	17	12	57	73	12	3.0	6.6	42	46%	.326
2020	SDN	MLB	24	2	3	0	23	5	43	46	8	2.7	6.3	30	43%	.282

Comparables: Aaron Civale, Taylor Rogers, Cy Sneed

Although the Padres were clearly committed to their young rotation last year, it was a shock when Margevicius broke camp with the big club. Until then, he'd never thrown a pitch above High-A ball. He rewarded their faith by posting a 1.69 ERA with a 12:1 whiff-to-walk rate over his first three starts, then faded badly and spent most of the year in Double-A where he belonged. Margevicius (pronounced "cuh-MAND-spesh-list") rarely dents 90 with his well-placed fastballs but fools the kids in the bus leagues with an intoxicating blend of sliders, changeups and looping low-70s benders. The best hitters in the world are better equipped to wait the young lefty out and grind his mundane stuff into batting practice fodder, but Margevicius has plenty of time to improve his high-wire act and could eventually earn a swingman's salary.

YEAR	TEAM	LVL	AGE	WHIP	ERA	DRA	WARP	MPH	FB%	WHF	CSP
2017	PDR	RK	21	1.21	1.42	2.48	0.7				
2017	TRI	A-	21	0.83	1.24	2.82	0.8				
2018	FTW	A	22	1.15	3.07	3.54	1.5				
2018	LEL	A+	22	1.31	4.30	4.61	0.5				
2019	AMA	AA	23	1.28	4.30	5.33	-0.3				
2019	SDN	MLB	23	1.61	6.79	6.97	-0.8	90.5	54.1	10.5	49.6
2020	SDN	MLB	24	1.35	4.99	5.24	0.2	90.3	55.7	10.9	51

Nick Margevicius, continued

Pitch Shape vs LHH

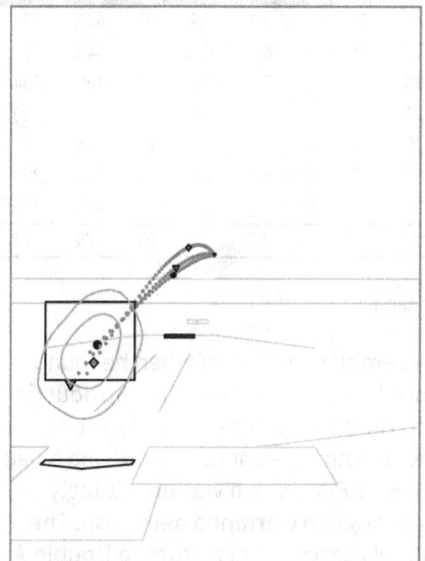

Pitch Shape vs RHH

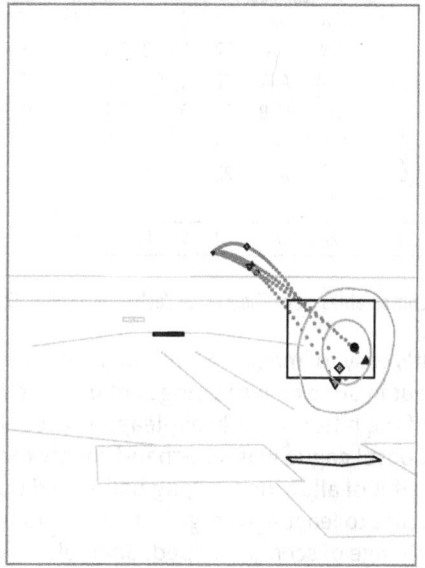

Type	Frequency	Velocity	H Movement	V Movement
● Fastball	54.1%	88.7 [89]	3.1 [117]	-15.5 [101]
☐ Sinker				
+ Cutter				
▲ Changeup	7.6%	79.3 [79]	4.3 [132]	-28.1 [98]
✕ Splitter				
▽ Slider	24.8%	80.6 [84]	-2.5 [90]	-36.3 [91]
◇ Curveball	13.5%	71.1 [75]	-5.5 [92]	-57.8 [78]
⊕ Slow Curveball				
✳ Knuckleball				
▼ Screwball				

Justus Sheffield LHP

Born: 05/13/96   Age: 24   Bats: L   Throws: L
Height: 6'0"   Weight: 200   Origin: Round 1, 2014 Draft (#31 overall)

YEAR	TEAM	LVL	AGE	W	L	SV	G	GS	IP	H	HR	BB/9	K/9	K	GB%	BABIP
2017	TRN	AA	21	7	6	0	17	17	93[1]	94	14	3.2	7.9	82	48%	.293
2018	TRN	AA	22	1	2	0	5	5	28	16	1	4.5	12.5	39	44%	.259
2018	SWB	AAA	22	6	4	0	20	15	88	66	3	3.7	8.6	84	46%	.264
2018	NYA	MLB	22	0	0	0	3	0	2[2]	4	1	10.1	0.0	0	55%	.300
2019	ARK	AA	23	5	3	0	12	12	78	62	4	2.1	9.8	85	44%	.293
2019	TAC	AAA	23	2	6	0	13	12	55	59	12	6.7	7.9	48	54%	.292
2019	SEA	MLB	23	0	1	0	8	7	36	44	5	4.5	9.2	37	54%	.375
2020	SEA	MLB	24	9	10	0	62	24	161	167	23	4.2	9.2	164	47%	.321

Comparables: Jake Thompson, Zack Littell, Robert Stephenson

It's easy to imagine Sheffield feeling some semblance of relief when he found out in June he was being sent down to Double-A from Tacoma. The introduction of the hitter-friendly big-league baseball to the already hitter-friendly Pacific Coast League was less-than-friendly to the southpaw. Poor command and a bad habit of allowing the long ball added up to 6.87 ERA, which was unsettlingly close to league average but still troubling enough to warrant a demotion. The change of scenery helped: Sheffield absolutely carved in his return to Double-A, posting the best FIP among all starters in the Texas League during his 12-start rejuvenation. A return to the big leagues in August yielded middling results, as his wipeout slider continued to wipe out good hitters while his low-spin fastball rarely missed any bats. Everyone knows there is impact bullpen potential if all else fails, but there's no rush for Seattle to resort to that backup plan any time soon. Besides, depending on how the offseason goes, he might be the team's fifth starter by default.

YEAR	TEAM	LVL	AGE	WHIP	ERA	DRA	WARP	MPH	FB%	WHF	CSP
2017	TRN	AA	21	1.36	3.18	5.33	-0.2				
2018	TRN	AA	22	1.07	2.25	3.54	0.6				
2018	SWB	AAA	22	1.16	2.56	3.41	2.1				
2018	NYA	MLB	22	2.62	10.12	6.56	-0.1	95.8	54.4	1.8	38.3
2019	ARK	AA	23	1.03	2.19	3.77	1.1				
2019	TAC	AAA	23	1.82	6.87	4.99	0.9				
2019	SEA	MLB	23	1.72	5.50	5.81	0.0	95.0	47.8	13.7	46.6
2020	SEA	MLB	24	1.50	5.02	4.93	1.0	94.9	49.6	13.3	44.2

Justus Sheffield, continued

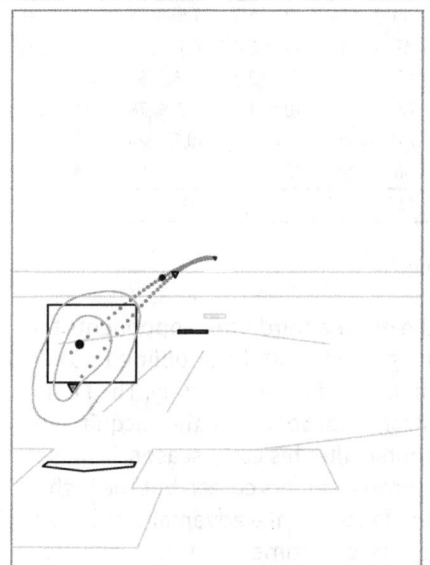
Pitch Shape vs LHH

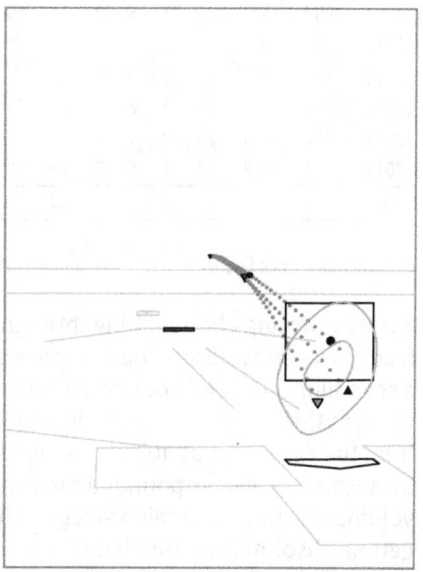
Pitch Shape vs RHH

Type	Frequency	Velocity	H Movement	V Movement
● Fastball	47.8%	93.1 [102]	6.5 [102]	-18.3 [94]
☐ Sinker				
+ Cutter				
▲ Changeup	16.7%	87.9 [110]	12.3 [95]	-29.5 [94]
✕ Splitter				
▽ Slider	35.6%	84.5 [100]	-3.4 [93]	-34.9 [95]
◇ Curveball				
⊕ Slow Curveball				
✱ Knuckleball				
▼ Screwball				

Seattle Mariners 2020

Erik Swanson RHP

Born: 09/04/93 Age: 26 Bats: R Throws: R
Height: 6'3" Weight: 235 Origin: Round 8, 2014 Draft (#246 overall)

YEAR	TEAM	LVL	AGE	W	L	SV	G	GS	IP	H	HR	BB/9	K/9	K	GB%	BABIP
2017	TAM	A+	23	7	3	0	20	20	100^1	115	10	1.3	7.5	84	42%	.344
2018	STA	A-	24	0	0	0	2	2	6^2	8	0	0.0	8.1	6	48%	.381
2018	TRN	AA	24	5	0	0	8	7	42^2	22	0	3.2	11.6	55	36%	.253
2018	SWB	AAA	24	3	2	0	14	13	72^1	63	10	1.7	9.7	78	37%	.283
2019	TAC	AAA	25	0	1	0	10	6	24^1	28	5	4.4	10.4	28	35%	.348
2019	SEA	MLB	25	1	5	2	27	8	58	56	17	1.9	8.1	52	38%	.241
2020	SEA	MLB	26	6	7	0	63	13	111	117	25	2.8	7.9	98	37%	.290

Comparables: Erick Fedde, Alec Mills, Brandon Workman

Forget worrying about getting through the order a third time—opponents that faced Swanson a *second* time in games he started posted a troubling 1.194 OPS, a scorching 554 points better than their first time facing the righty. The Mariners thought they may have starter ingredients in Swanson when they acquired him from the Yankees, but quickly changed course after his early-season struggles. Swanson had always pounded the zone throughout his career, but the high volume of strikes that minor-league hitters failed to take advantage of were getting absolutely pummeled by big leaguers, oftentimes over the fence. He remains dangerously homer-prone, but otherwise improved across the board once he moved to the bullpen, suggesting a respectable future as a decent middle-relief option.

YEAR	TEAM	LVL	AGE	WHIP	ERA	DRA	WARP	MPH	FB%	WHF	CSP
2017	TAM	A+	23	1.29	3.95	4.53	0.9				
2018	STA	A-	24	1.20	4.05	4.42	0.1				
2018	TRN	AA	24	0.87	0.42	2.24	1.5				
2018	SWB	AAA	24	1.06	3.86	3.85	1.4				
2019	TAC	AAA	25	1.64	5.55	5.57	0.2				
2019	SEA	MLB	25	1.17	5.74	5.91	-0.2	95.2	67.9	11.2	49.2
2020	SEA	MLB	26	1.36	5.20	5.28	0.2	94.8	69.1	11.4	50.1

Erik Swanson, continued

Pitch Shape vs LHH

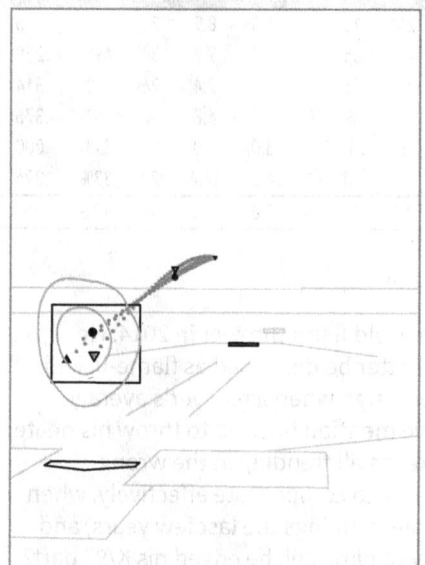

Pitch Shape vs RHH

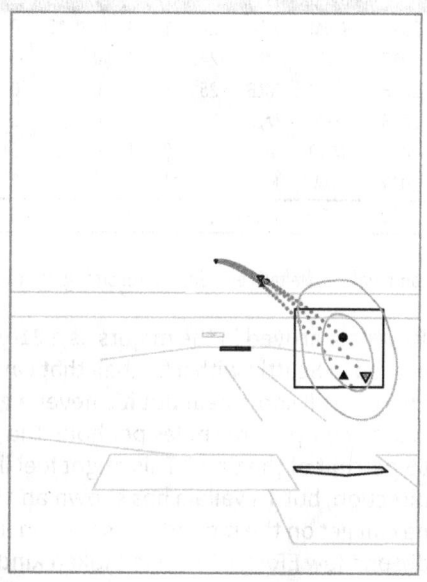

Type	Frequency	Velocity	H Movement	V Movement
● Fastball	67.9%	93.2 [102]	-7.2 [98]	-11.8 [111]
☐ Sinker				
+ Cutter				
▲ Changeup	15.1%	86.2 [104]	-8.2 [114]	-22.5 [114]
✕ Splitter				
▽ Slider	17.0%	85.8 [106]	3.4 [93]	-29.3 [111]
◇ Curveball				
✦ Slow Curveball				
✳ Knuckleball				
▼ Screwball				

Seattle Mariners 2020

Sam Tuivailala RHP

Born: 10/19/92 Age: 27 Bats: R Throws: R
Height: 6'3" Weight: 225 Origin: Round 3, 2010 Draft (#106 overall)

YEAR	TEAM	LVL	AGE	W	L	SV	G	GS	IP	H	HR	BB/9	K/9	K	GB%	BABIP
2017	MEM	AAA	24	1	0	6	18	0	21^1	13	2	1.3	8.9	21	42%	.216
2017	SLN	MLB	24	3	3	0	37	0	42^1	35	4	2.3	7.2	34	49%	.258
2018	SLN	MLB	25	3	3	0	31	0	31^2	35	3	3.1	7.4	26	50%	.314
2018	SEA	MLB	25	1	0	0	5	0	5^1	6	0	1.7	6.8	4	56%	.375
2019	MOD	A+	26	0	1	0	6	0	6	1	1	3.0	9.0	6	31%	.000
2019	SEA	MLB	26	1	0	0	23	2	23	13	1	4.3	10.6	27	33%	.226
2020	SEA	MLB	27	3	3	7	53	3	56	53	8	3.6	9.0	56	42%	.292

Comparables: Neftalí Feliz, Shawn Armstrong, Bruce Rondón

Tuivailala arrived in the majors as a 21-year-old flamethrower in 2014. He arrived in Seattle with a fastball that can better be described as flame-licked. There is still some heat but it's never a good sign when a reliever's average velocity drops three miles per hour. Did we mention he used to throw his heater 65 percent of the time? This might feel like it's all trending in the wrong direction, but Tuivailala has shown an ability to compensate effectively, when he can get on the mound. He's thrown limited innings the last few years, and despite low ERAs, DRA hasn't taken kindly to him. still, he edged his K/9" part? "Still, even with decreased velocity, Tui might have carved a path forward in the majors on the back of a diversified pitch mix: he didn't throw any individual pitch over 35 percent of the time, and consequently edged his K/9 into the double digits for the first time since 2015.

YEAR	TEAM	LVL	AGE	WHIP	ERA	DRA	WARP	MPH	FB%	WHF	CSP
2017	MEM	AAA	24	0.75	1.27	1.77	0.8				
2017	SLN	MLB	24	1.09	2.55	3.86	0.6	97.8	61.8	11	54
2018	SLN	MLB	25	1.45	3.69	4.77	0.1	97.6	58.7	10.6	52.3
2018	SEA	MLB	25	1.31	1.69	2.93	0.1	96.8	63	13.6	53.9
2019	MOD	A+	26	0.50	1.50	2.94	0.1				
2019	SEA	MLB	26	1.04	2.35	4.69	0.2	95.1	62	11.7	44
2020	SEA	MLB	27	1.34	4.38	4.46	0.5	96.4	61.5	11.4	49.9

Sam Tuivailala, continued

Pitch Shape vs LHH

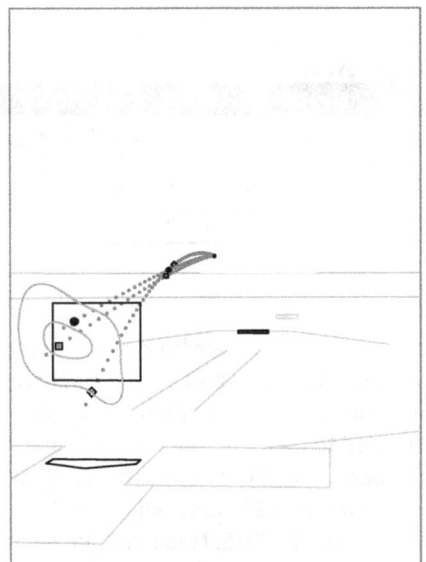

Pitch Shape vs RHH

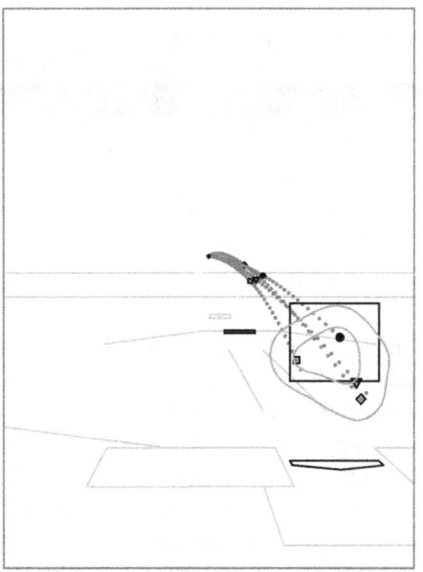

Type	Frequency	Velocity	H Movement	V Movement
● Fastball	34.9%	93.8 [104]	-9 [90]	-15.3 [102]
☐ Sinker	27.0%	93.5 [105]	-14.3 [89]	-20 [101]
+ Cutter				
▲ Changeup				
✕ Splitter				
▽ Slider	20.2%	87.1 [111]	2.4 [89]	-27.3 [117]
◇ Curveball	17.9%	79 [101]	10.3 [111]	-47.4 [100]
⊕ Slow Curveball				
✳ Knuckleball				
▼ Screwball				

PLAYER COMMENTS WITHOUT GRAPHS

Eric Filia OF
Born: 07/06/92 Age: 27 Bats: L Throws: R
Height: 6'0" Weight: 189 Origin: Round 20, 2016 Draft (#597 overall)

YEAR	TEAM	LVL	AGE	PA	R	2B	3B	HR	RBI	BB	K	SB	CS	AVG/OBP/SLG
2017	MOD	A+	24	567	63	28	5	5	59	65	45	9	6	.326/.407/.434
2018	ARK	AA	25	345	44	14	1	2	38	44	30	1	0	.274/.371/.348
2019	TAC	AAA	26	151	24	13	0	2	13	25	15	0	0	.331/.450/.488
2020	SEA	MLB	27	251	25	12	1	4	25	27	34	1	0	.259/.345/.376

Comparables: Daniel Robertson, Raffy Lopez, Nick Martini

On July 6, 1992, two future professional baseball players were born on opposite sides of the country: Filia, in Huntington Beach, California, and Manny Machado, in the Miami suburb of Hialeah. Since that summer day, Machado raced to the big leagues in a relative blink while Filia decided to take the route that Google Maps fails to mention includes some forest roads. Call it the scenic route, if you will. In 2012, Machado made his major-league debut at 20 years old while Filia was a bench bat at UCLA as a 19-year-old freshman. In 2015, Machado played in 162 Major League games while Filia played in 0 NCAA games due to an academic suspension. In 2019, Machado signed a $300 million free agent contract while Filia received a suspension for a "drug of abuse"—the second of his Minor League career—costing him the first 100 games of the season. And yet, thanks to an advanced hit tool that has remained throughout the bumpy, off-road journey, Filia still has the chance to share a big-league field with Machado one day.

YEAR	TEAM	LVL	AGE	PA	DRC+	VORP	BABIP	BRR	FRAA	WARP
2017	MOD	A+	24	567	150	39.8	.348	-0.6	RF(106): -11.7, 1B(12): -1.0	2.5
2018	ARK	AA	25	345	109	5.1	.297	-1.1	RF(44): -0.9, LF(11): -0.8	0.6
2019	TAC	AAA	26	151	144	10.0	.358	-1.5	RF(15): -1.4, 1B(14): -1.0	0.6
2020	SEA	MLB	27	251	97	6.7	.290	-0.3	RF -1, 1B -1	0.5

Jake Fraley CF

Born: 05/25/95 Age: 25 Bats: L Throws: L
Height: 6'0" Weight: 195 Origin: Round 2, 2016 Draft (#77 overall)

YEAR	TEAM	LVL	AGE	PA	R	2B	3B	HR	RBI	BB	K	SB	CS	AVG/OBP/SLG
2017	PCH	A+	22	105	6	3	1	1	12	7	24	1	3	.170/.238/.255
2018	PCH	A+	23	260	39	19	7	4	41	26	44	11	8	.347/.415/.547
2019	ARK	AA	24	259	40	15	2	11	47	23	55	16	5	.313/.386/.539
2019	TAC	AAA	24	168	28	12	3	8	33	11	34	6	2	.276/.333/.553
2019	SEA	MLB	24	41	3	2	0	0	1	0	14	0	0	.150/.171/.200
2020	*SEA*	*MLB*	*25*	*350*	*39*	*14*	*3*	*13*	*43*	*22*	*92*	*14*	*7*	*.233/.291/.411*

Comparables: Rip Repulski, Roy Sievers, Anthony Gose

Upon acquiring Fraley from Tampa Bay in one of the team's ritual solstice exchanges, the Mariners organization remarked that the LSU product had made a mechanical tweak that piqued their interest, in the vein of Mitch Haniger. His mini-breakout in the Florida State League in 2018 became a much larger coming-out party in 2019, which saw Fraley absolutely torch the Texas League, and hit well enough in Tacoma to make his major-league debut in August. Injuries continued to haunt Fraley, as they have throughout his pro career, and appeared to hamper his first dozen big-league games before the Mariners shut him down for the season. If he can stay on the field, he may now be able to convincingly outplay the dreaded "fourth outfielder" label.

YEAR	TEAM	LVL	AGE	PA	DRC+	VORP	BABIP	BRR	FRAA	WARP
2017	PCH	A+	22	105	36	-5.0	.211	-0.6	CF(26): -3.6	-0.7
2018	PCH	A+	23	260	169	26.4	.407	-2.2	LF(31): 2.6, CF(21): 2.1	2.7
2019	ARK	AA	24	259	191	35.6	.370	-0.3	RF(21): -1.3, LF(12): -1.1	2.1
2019	TAC	AAA	24	168	103	11.2	.304	-1.3	CF(21): 0.9, RF(9): -0.7	0.5
2019	SEA	MLB	24	41	64	-0.6	.231	-0.7	CF(11): -1.5, RF(1): 0.0	-0.3
2020	*SEA*	*MLB*	*25*	*350*	*87*	*3.7*	*.285*	*0.7*	*CF 0, RF 1*	*0.4*

Jarred Kelenic   OF

Born: 07/16/99   Age: 20   Bats: L   Throws: L
Height: 6'0"   Weight: 196   Origin: Round 1, 2018 Draft (#6 overall)

YEAR	TEAM	LVL	AGE	PA	R	2B	3B	HR	RBI	BB	K	SB	CS	AVG/OBP/SLG
2018	MTS	RK	18	51	9	2	2	1	9	4	11	4	0	.413/.451/.609
2018	KNG	RK	18	200	33	8	4	5	33	22	39	11	1	.253/.350/.431
2019	WVA	A	19	218	33	14	3	11	29	25	45	7	4	.309/.394/.586
2019	MOD	A+	19	190	36	13	1	6	22	17	49	10	3	.290/.353/.485
2019	ARK	AA	19	92	11	4	1	6	17	8	17	3	0	.253/.315/.542
2020	SEA	MLB	20	251	29	12	1	11	34	19	69	3	1	.245/.307/.453

Comparables: Ronald Acuña Jr., Byron Buxton, Corey Seager

It all happened so fast. He wasn't even a Met long enough for the fans to know how to pronounce his name; "I can't believe we gave up kuh-LEH-nick" or "oh God, kel-nitch is going to be an All-Star, what is Brodie thinking?" (It's KELL-nick). And yet, for all the cries of front office malpractice when Kelenic was shipped to Seattle in the Robinson Canó/Edwin Díaz blockbuster, few could have foreseen how quickly the prospect huggers would chalk this up as a certified catastrophe for the Mets. Fans suffered through Canó injury updates and Díaz blown saves only to receive the frequent double whammy of opening Twitter to see the Wisconsin native's latest exploits, which included: participating in the All-Star Futures Game, reaching Double-A in his first full season and being the youngest player in the minors to go 20-20. Detractors may argue that Kelenic still doesn't have one plus-plus tool in his profile, but he's about as well-rounded of an outfield prospect as you're going to see. Even the most optimistic of big-league ETAs for high school hitters are rarely projected as any earlier than the player's first legal drink, but Kelenic doesn't appear to be constrained by traditional timetables. Service time games be damned; he could be knocking on the door ready to enter the major league party by the end of 2020.

YEAR	TEAM	LVL	AGE	PA	DRC+	VORP	BABIP	BRR	FRAA	WARP
2018	MTS	RK	18	51	183	8.0	.514	-0.1	CF(9): 2.0	0.7
2018	KNG	RK	18	200	120	15.2	.300	2.5	CF(43): 5.8	1.9
2019	WVA	A	19	218	181	25.6	.356	-0.5	CF(33): -1.8, RF(8): -0.1	2.3
2019	MOD	A+	19	190	138	17.7	.368	1.4	CF(32): 1.1, RF(8): -1.2	1.3
2019	ARK	AA	19	92	134	9.0	.246	0.6	CF(12): 0.6, RF(5): 0.6	0.7
2020	SEA	MLB	20	251	99	8.1	.303	0.3	CF -1, RF -1	0.6

Cal Raleigh C

Born: 11/26/96 Age: 23 Bats: B Throws: R
Height: 6'3" Weight: 215 Origin: Round 3, 2018 Draft (#90 overall)

YEAR	TEAM	LVL	AGE	PA	R	2B	3B	HR	RBI	BB	K	SB	CS	AVG/OBP/SLG
2018	EVE	A-	21	167	25	10	1	8	29	18	29	1	1	.288/.367/.534
2019	MOD	A+	22	348	48	19	0	22	66	33	69	4	0	.261/.336/.535
2019	ARK	AA	22	159	16	6	0	7	16	14	47	0	0	.228/.296/.414
2020	SEA	MLB	23	251	32	12	0	14	39	17	71	1	0	.239/.295/.481

Comparables: Chris Shaw, Josh Donaldson, Travis Shaw

YEAR	TEAM	P. COUNT	FRM RUNS	BLK RUNS	THRW RUNS	TOT RUNS
2019	ARK	3199	1.0	0.0	-1.4	-0.5
2020	SEA	9182	-1.7	-0.5	-1.3	-3.5

A fast-moving, highly-drafted, offensive catcher from a college baseball powerhouse in Florida who grew up in a baseball family? It's a familiar story for Mariners fans, but certainly an unfair comparison between how we should project Raleigh and the ultimately disappointing tenure of Mike Zunino. The expectations for a third-overall pick and third-round selection differ significantly, but the current front office may still keep Zunino's cautionary developmental tale in mind as they bring Raleigh along. The switch-hitting backstop's first full season gave even the most conservative of prospect observers a lot to love. He swatted more dingers than any other catcher in the minors, including a 9-in-11-games tear in July which essentially forced a promotion to Double-A. The bat cooled off in Arkansas, where it wouldn't be surprising to see him spend a considerable amount of time over the next season or two, getting more reps against left-handed pitching and continuing to improve his defense. With the team still a year or two away from really Going For It, Raleigh can take his sweet time.

YEAR	TEAM	LVL	AGE	PA	DRC+	VORP	BABIP	BRR	FRAA	WARP
2018	EVE	A-	21	167	141	11.7	.309	0.3	C(25): -0.2	1.2
2019	MOD	A+	22	348	151	33.4	.267	0.8	C(55): 0.9	3.1
2019	ARK	AA	22	159	108	7.5	.286	-0.6	C(26): 0.0	0.6
2020	SEA	MLB	23	251	101	7.9	.278	-0.5	C -3	0.5

Julio Rodriguez OF

Born: 12/29/00 Age: 19 Bats: R Throws: R
Height: 6'4" Weight: 225 Origin: International Free Agent, 2017

YEAR	TEAM	LVL	AGE	PA	R	2B	3B	HR	RBI	BB	K	SB	CS	AVG/OBP/SLG
2018	DMR	RK	17	255	50	13	9	5	36	30	40	10	0	.315/.404/.525
2019	WVA	A	18	295	50	20	1	10	50	20	66	1	3	.293/.359/.490
2019	MOD	A+	18	72	13	6	3	2	19	5	10	0	0	.462/.514/.738
2020	SEA	MLB	19	251	26	13	2	7	29	19	65	1	0	.254/.322/.414

Comparables: Nomar Mazara, Vladimir Guerrero Jr., Jon Singleton

It was a summer of hyperbole for Rodriguez, who began the year as one of the youngest players in full-season ball and finished it as the youngest player in the Arizona Fall League. Only a broken hand via hit-by-pitch that cost Rodriguez two months could slow him down, as his excellent, albeit abbreviated, South Atlantic League stint was convincing enough to earn an August promotion. He joined uber-prospect Wander Franco as the only 18-year-old in High-A, where he continued to show out. His listed height and weight undersell his gigantic frame, which will likely move out of center field eventually, though his athleticism and plus arm should make him above-average in a corner. Rodriguez endearingly toes the delicate line between confidence and cockiness, routinely hashtagging his own highlights on social media with #JRODshow. It's a nickname he's embraced to honor his favorite player, Alex Rodríguez, who dominated the sport in a way he unabashedly aspires to mirror one day. Phenoms like Juan Soto have shown that with the right combination of maturity, poise, and extraordinary raw ability, players can dictate their own timelines. So many things have to go right for a player to make his big-league debut as a teenager, but Rodriguez, who will play all of 2020 at 19, sure does check a lot of boxes. There is hardly any rush from the franchise's standpoint, but The J-Rod Show might be closer to airing on a major network sooner rather than later.

YEAR	TEAM	LVL	AGE	PA	DRC+	VORP	BABIP	BRR	FRAA	WARP
2018	DMR	RK	17	255	163	34.0	.364	0.6	RF(45): 8.1, CF(6): -0.1	2.9
2019	WVA	A	18	295	160	27.7	.353	0.0	RF(40): 4.7, CF(22): -0.2	2.8
2019	MOD	A+	18	72	254	17.2	.528	0.5	CF(13): -3.4, RF(3): -0.5	0.9
2020	SEA	MLB	19	251	98	7.4	.327	-0.2	RF 1, CF -1	0.8

Jose Siri CF

Born: 07/22/95 Age: 24 Bats: R Throws: R
Height: 6'2" Weight: 175 Origin: International Free Agent, 2012

YEAR	TEAM	LVL	AGE	PA	R	2B	3B	HR	RBI	BB	K	SB	CS	AVG/OBP/SLG
2017	DYT	A	21	552	92	24	11	24	76	33	130	46	12	.293/.341/.530
2018	DAY	A+	22	126	15	9	2	1	9	4	32	9	1	.261/.280/.395
2018	PEN	AA	22	283	42	8	9	12	34	24	91	14	5	.229/.300/.474
2019	CHT	AA	23	405	46	15	1	11	50	33	126	21	6	.251/.313/.388
2019	LOU	AAA	23	112	10	4	1	0	3	9	39	5	2	.186/.252/.245
2020	CIN	MLB	24	35	4	2	0	1	4	2	13	1	1	.224/.272/.389

Comparables: Zoilo Almonte, Jeremy Moore, Aristides Aquino

A center fielder with power and speed is one of the most exciting archetypes in baseball. When it clicks, the profile can result in all-star or all-time great levels of production. Siri has plenty of athleticism and physicality to burn but almost zero production to show for it all. Put simply, he strikes out too often to leverage his gifts. He's tried to adjust and it hasn't worked. The Reds have promoted him and that hasn't worked, either. Siri will probably get big-league burn and, who knows, maybe somehow he'll unlock his immense potential. Based on everything we know about Siri and his career, Houdini himself would find that to be a trick beyond comprehension.

YEAR	TEAM	LVL	AGE	PA	DRC+	VORP	BABIP	BRR	FRAA	WARP
2017	DYT	A	21	552	137	50.5	.349	7.4	CF(103): 15.7, RF(9): 1.5	6.4
2018	DAY	A+	22	126	89	2.2	.341	1.1	CF(26): 0.4	0.4
2018	PEN	AA	22	283	91	15.0	.301	2.2	CF(59): -3.9	0.5
2019	CHT	AA	23	405	84	8.0	.349	-0.1	CF(98): 22.8, RF(1): 0.0	3.2
2019	LOU	AAA	23	112	42	-6.0	.302	1.6	CF(26): 2.3, RF(4): -0.1	0.0
2020	CIN	MLB	24	35	70	0.0	.332	0.1	CF 1	0.1

Donnie Walton INF

Born: 05/25/94   Age: 26   Bats: L   Throws: R
Height: 5'10"   Weight: 184   Origin: Round 5, 2016 Draft (#147 overall)

YEAR	TEAM	LVL	AGE	PA	R	2B	3B	HR	RBI	BB	K	SB	CS	AVG/OBP/SLG
2017	MOD	A+	23	272	37	16	1	2	24	27	49	6	6	.269/.349/.368
2018	MOD	A+	24	256	35	12	3	3	19	30	37	8	3	.309/.402/.433
2018	ARK	AA	24	238	22	14	1	1	22	21	34	3	1	.236/.325/.327
2019	ARK	AA	25	558	72	22	3	11	50	63	72	10	13	.300/.390/.427
2019	SEA	MLB	25	19	2	0	0	0	2	3	5	0	1	.188/.316/.188
2020	SEA	MLB	26	70	7	3	0	1	7	6	14	1	0	.247/.318/.365

Comparables: Dean Anna, Robinson Chirinos, J.P. Crawford

Pick your favorite platitude about gritty, scrappy, hard-nosed, *voice gets a bit more gravelly* BASEBALL PLAYERS and it has probably been ascribed to Walton at some point. You should expect nothing less for an undersized middle infielder whose dad, a former minor leaguer, coached him for four years (you're damn right he went back for his senior year) at Oklahoma State. It's honestly a miracle he doesn't play for the Cardinals. And yet, 2019 saw Walton take statistical strides beyond what you might expect from a player of his clichéd caliber, as he hit legitimately well in a full season in the Texas League, albeit as a 25-year-old in Double-A. Unlikely to be a core part of the Next Good Mariners Team, it's still easy to see Walton sticking around as a Triple-A shuttle bus utility infielder candidate.

YEAR	TEAM	LVL	AGE	PA	DRC+	VORP	BABIP	BRR	FRAA	WARP
2017	MOD	A+	23	272	110	4.4	.330	-4.2	SS(47): 9.3, 2B(16): 1.7	2.0
2018	MOD	A+	24	256	147	24.2	.358	-0.3	2B(36): -4.2, SS(19): 1.0	1.7
2018	ARK	AA	24	238	83	1.8	.276	-1.4	2B(62): 6.2	0.8
2019	ARK	AA	25	558	159	60.3	.333	-2.0	SS(102): 12.4, 2B(19): 1.6	6.6
2019	SEA	MLB	25	19	83	0.5	.273	-0.2	SS(5): -0.7, 2B(2): -0.5	-0.1
2020	SEA	MLB	26	70	85	1.2	.295	-0.2	2B 0, SS 1	0.2

Evan White 1B

Born: 04/26/96 Age: 24 Bats: R Throws: L
Height: 6'3" Weight: 205 Origin: Round 1, 2017 Draft (#17 overall)

YEAR	TEAM	LVL	AGE	PA	R	2B	3B	HR	RBI	BB	K	SB	CS	AVG/OBP/SLG
2017	EVE	A-	21	55	6	1	1	3	12	6	6	1	1	.277/.345/.532
2018	MOD	A+	22	538	72	27	7	11	66	52	103	4	3	.303/.375/.458
2019	ARK	AA	23	400	61	13	2	18	55	29	92	2	0	.293/.350/.488
2020	SEA	MLB	24	385	45	16	2	17	53	23	105	0	0	.261/.310/.457

Comparables: Matt Clark, Rhys Hoskins, Kevin Cron

There's only so much you can do to make a first base prospect literally named "White" interesting. Give this one credit, though, as the 2017 first-round pick has managed to spice up his prospect profile beyond its vanilla exterior. To start, he has made first base defense look cooler than it has any right to be, with scouts consistently lauding his athleticism around the bag from stretches to scoops to plays you hadn't even thought possible. Of course, there is no level of first base defense that would actually carry a player to the big leagues, which makes White's continued progress with the bat all the more crucial. A minor swing tweak towards the end of 2018 carried over into his first go at Double-A, where he was one of the most productive hitters at the level, matching high exit velos with an increased proclivity for lifting the ball. He might not get the chance to replicate the achievement in Triple-A Tacoma: the Mariners signed White to a six-year, $24 million pact in late November, removing any concerns over service time, and have declared that he'll have every chance to win the first-base job in spring.

YEAR	TEAM	LVL	AGE	PA	DRC+	VORP	BABIP	BRR	FRAA	WARP
2017	EVE	A-	21	55	122	3.7	.250	-0.1	1B(8): -0.6	0.1
2018	MOD	A+	22	538	143	38.4	.363	-0.5	1B(106): 5.5	3.5
2019	ARK	AA	23	400	153	32.0	.346	1.1	1B(88): -5.3	1.9
2020	SEA	MLB	24	385	103	8.3	.323	-0.6	1B -1	0.7

Logan Gilbert RHP

Born: 05/05/97 Age: 23 Bats: R Throws: R
Height: 6'6" Weight: 225 Origin: Round 1, 2018 Draft (#14 overall)

YEAR	TEAM	LVL	AGE	W	L	SV	G	GS	IP	H	HR	BB/9	K/9	K	GB%	BABIP
2019	WVA	A	22	1	0	0	5	5	22²	9	2	2.4	14.3	36	22%	.184
2019	MOD	A+	22	5	3	0	12	12	62¹	52	3	1.7	10.5	73	47%	.320
2019	ARK	AA	22	4	2	0	9	9	50	34	2	2.7	10.1	56	33%	.271
2020	SEA	MLB	23	2	2	0	33	0	35	35	5	3.4	10.0	39	36%	.319

Comparables: Ryan Helsley, Matt Harvey, Ben Lively

Gilbert appears to be on a faster track to the big leagues than the gradual routes taken by fellow Stetson University alumni Jacob deGrom and Corey Kluber, neither of whom cracked the majors until after their 25th birthdays. After a full-season debut that stretched across three levels, the latest hard-throwing Hatter may be primed to reach the bigs before he even turns 24. The mid-90s velocity that put him on the national radar in the Cape returned and held steady, he continued to throw a ton of strikes, and he stayed healthy. This is exactly what it's supposed to look like when you draft an advanced college pitcher, checking all the boxes of what would be considered a best case scenario for Year 1. Gilbert still tends to be labeled more starter than star, but as deGrom and Kluber have shown, there is a well-traveled road from DeLand to the Cy Young. Gilbert has taken all the right steps so far.

YEAR	TEAM	LVL	AGE	WHIP	ERA	DRA	WARP	MPH	FB%	WHF	CSP
2019	WVA	A	22	0.66	1.59	1.53	1.0				
2019	MOD	A+	22	1.03	1.73	3.20	1.4				
2019	ARK	AA	22	0.98	2.88	3.57	0.8				
2020	SEA	MLB	23	1.37	4.57	4.61	0.2				

Kendall Graveman RHP

Born: 12/21/90 Age: 29 Bats: R Throws: R
Height: 6'2" Weight: 200 Origin: Round 8, 2013 Draft (#235 overall)

YEAR	TEAM	LVL	AGE	W	L	SV	G	GS	IP	H	HR	BB/9	K/9	K	GB%	BABIP
2017	NAS	AAA	26	0	1	0	3	3	10	18	1	3.6	6.3	7	46%	.425
2017	OAK	MLB	26	6	4	0	19	19	105^1	114	12	2.7	6.0	70	52%	.313
2018	NAS	AAA	27	2	1	0	4	4	24	35	3	2.6	6.0	16	56%	.405
2018	OAK	MLB	27	1	5	0	7	7	34^1	44	9	3.4	7.1	27	57%	.324
2020	SEA	MLB	29	5	7	0	19	19	87	104	18	3.0	6.9	67	52%	.315

Comparables: Joe Kelly, José Ureña, Jake Buchanan

Just for fun, picture Graveman walking into a room and boasting that he was once traded for prime Josh Donaldson. To this point—and likely to any point in the future—that's his claim to fame. The Cubs didn't see enough during his recovery from Tommy John surgery to justify picking up his option. The Mariners evidently did, signing Graveman to a big-league deal where he should get a crack at the majors, the way most every other pitcher in that system did in 2019.

YEAR	TEAM	LVL	AGE	WHIP	ERA	DRA	WARP	MPH	FB%	WHF	CSP
2017	NAS	AAA	26	2.20	7.20	7.52	-0.2				
2017	OAK	MLB	26	1.39	4.19	5.42	0.2	95.8	68.9	7.4	43.4
2018	NAS	AAA	27	1.75	4.50	7.26	-0.5				
2018	OAK	MLB	27	1.66	7.60	5.38	0.0	96.2	57.2	8	44.4
2020	SEA	MLB	29	1.53	5.92	5.73	-0.1	95.2	65	7.6	44

George Kirby RHP

Born: 02/04/98 Age: 22 Bats: R Throws: R
Height: 6'4" Weight: 201 Origin: Round 1, 2019 Draft (#20 overall)

YEAR	TEAM	LVL	AGE	W	L	SV	G	GS	IP	H	HR	BB/9	K/9	K	GB%	BABIP
2019	EVE	A-	21	0	0	0	9	8	23	24	1	0.0	9.8	25	48%	.355
2020	SEA	MLB	22	2	2	0	33	0	35	35	5	3.5	7.4	29	42%	.286

Comparables: Andrew Moore, Joe Musgrove, Pat Light

The Mariners went back to the mid-major college starter well for their first-round pick in 2019. A year after selecting Stetson's Logan Gilbert, Seattle popped Kirby out of Elon University with the 20th-overall selection. Kirby's first-round pedigree was built on a mid-90s fastball, a curveball that flashes plus, and an extreme propensity to not throw four balls during an at-bat. He allowed one free pass in his breakout summer on the Cape (to fellow 2019 first-rounder Michael Busch), just six walks next to 106 strikeouts in his draft spring at Elon, and zero in his first 23 pro innings after signing. There have been a fair share of highly-drafted collegiate no-walk artists in recent years, but their success levels in pro ball have varied from back-end emergency starter Tom Eshelman to All-Star Game MVP Shane Bieber. Kirby's raw stuff more closely resembles the latter's, but he'll have to show it plays against more than just the Colonial Athletic Association or the Northwest League before he sniffs any Top 100 lists.

YEAR	TEAM	LVL	AGE	WHIP	ERA	DRA	WARP	MPH	FB%	WHF	CSP
2019	EVE	A-	21	1.04	2.35	3.50	0.5				
2020	SEA	MLB	22	1.38	4.65	4.75	0.2				

Juan Then RHP

Born: 02/07/00 Age: 20 Bats: R Throws: R
Height: 6'1" Weight: 155 Origin: International Free Agent, 2016

YEAR	TEAM	LVL	AGE	W	L	SV	G	GS	IP	H	HR	BB/9	K/9	K	GB%	BABIP
2017	DMR	RK	17	2	2	0	13	13	61[1]	50	3	2.2	8.2	56	54%	.278
2018	YAN	RK	18	0	3	0	11	11	50	38	2	2.0	7.6	42	48%	.259
2019	EVE	A-	19	0	3	0	7	6	30[1]	24	1	2.7	9.5	32	36%	.299
2019	WVA	A	19	1	2	0	3	3	16	7	1	2.2	7.9	14	32%	.150
2020	SEA	MLB	20	2	2	0	33	0	35	35	5	3.8	7.5	29	34%	.291

Comparables: Felix Jorge, Jose Suarez, Huascar Ynoa

At first, Juan was a Mariner, signed as a promising 16-year-old right-hander out of the Dominican Republic. Then, Juan was a Yankee, traded away for Literally Nick Rumbelow. Then, Juan became a Mariner again, the return for half a season of Edwin Encarnación. This string of terrible puns falls apart when we inform you that it's actually pronounced 'ten.' But one *could* say that Juan Then made his full-season debut at Low-A West Virginia as one of the Then-youngest pitchers in the Sally League and more than held his own. We may never know what Then learned at Yankees summer camp but he clearly developed enough to warrant re-acquiring, and now looks like another name to monitor in a system suddenly flush with projectable arms. His improvements have already made him Juan-Thenth of a Mariners Top 10 list.

YEAR	TEAM	LVL	AGE	WHIP	ERA	DRA	WARP	MPH	FB%	WHF	CSP
2017	DMR	RK	17	1.06	2.64	1.91	2.7				
2018	YAN	RK	18	0.98	2.70	2.07	2.1				
2019	EVE	A-	19	1.09	3.56	3.17	0.7				
2019	WVA	A	19	0.69	2.25	2.90	0.4				
2020	SEA	MLB	20	1.42	4.81	4.84	0.1				

Taijuan Walker RHP
Born: 08/13/92 Age: 27 Bats: R Throws: R
Height: 6'4" Weight: 235 Origin: Round 1, 2010 Draft (#43 overall)

YEAR	TEAM	LVL	AGE	W	L	SV	G	GS	IP	H	HR	BB/9	K/9	K	GB%	BABIP
2017	ARI	MLB	24	9	9	0	28	28	157^1	148	17	3.5	8.4	146	50%	.291
2018	ARI	MLB	25	0	0	0	3	3	13	15	1	3.5	6.2	9	45%	.341
2019	ARI	MLB	26	0	0	0	1	1	1	1	0	0.0	9.0	1	33%	.333
2020	ARI	MLB	27	2	2	0	33	0	35	36	5	3.6	7.2	28	39%	.296

Comparables: Julio Teheran, Tyler Skaggs, Matt Cain

The "most hyped finale" award of 2019 goes to *Game of Thrones*. Coming in second place was the final game of the Diamondbacks' season, in which they trotted out Walker to make his first start since undergoing Tommy John surgery in early 2018. Like the show, Walker continues to entice both fans with his "what's going to happen next?" potential. Also like the show, given years of unfulfilled hype, it seems increasingly likely we'll be left scratching our heads and wondering what the hell happened. Something we do know? Walker's time with the Diamondbacks and *Game of Thrones* both came to an unsatisfying close in 2019.

YEAR	TEAM	LVL	AGE	WHIP	ERA	DRA	WARP	MPH	FB%	WHF	CSP
2017	ARI	MLB	24	1.33	3.49	4.90	1.2	95.9	59.1	9.7	46.7
2018	ARI	MLB	25	1.54	3.46	5.15	0.0	96.5	70.5	7.1	53.8
2019	ARI	MLB	26	1.00	0.00			94.3	66.7	13.3	43.8
2020	ARI	MLB	27	1.41	4.74	4.80	0.2	95.5	61	9.6	48.4

Art Warren   RHP
Born: 03/23/93   Age: 27   Bats: R   Throws: R
Height: 6'3"   Weight: 230   Origin: Round 23, 2015 Draft (#695 overall)

YEAR	TEAM	LVL	AGE	W	L	SV	G	GS	IP	H	HR	BB/9	K/9	K	GB%	BABIP
2017	MOD	A+	24	3	1	8	43	0	64²	58	5	3.5	9.3	67	45%	.312
2018	ARK	AA	25	1	2	2	14	0	15²	10	0	8.0	12.6	22	39%	.303
2019	ARK	AA	26	2	1	15	29	0	31²	23	1	3.7	11.7	41	60%	.310
2019	SEA	MLB	26	1	0	0	6	0	5¹	2	0	3.4	8.4	5	29%	.143
2020	SEA	MLB	27	1	1	0	25	0	26	28	5	4.8	7.0	20	45%	.293

Comparables: Kyle Dowdy, Jon Meloan, Brad Wieck

Every day, Twitter users solicit the wisdom of @ArtDecider—an anonymous account that serves up definitive rulings on whether something is Art or Not Art—to determine whether various people, places, images, videos, memes, or otherwise are, indeed, Art. The account then renders a one- or two-word judgment that settles the inquiry once and for all. In the case of Warren, there isn't much to decide: his name is Art, so he is Art, not Arthur, and the first big-leaguer to go by Art since Art Howe in 1985. Whether Warren will be asked to fill the bona fide-closer role in which he has served throughout the minors or as a big-stuff middle reliever with fringy command isn't up to us. Check in with @ReliefRoleDecider. Or Scott Servais.

YEAR	TEAM	LVL	AGE	WHIP	ERA	DRA	WARP	MPH	FB%	WHF	CSP
2017	MOD	A+	24	1.28	3.06	4.50	0.3				
2018	ARK	AA	25	1.53	1.72	4.44	0.1				
2019	ARK	AA	26	1.14	1.71	3.41	0.5				
2019	SEA	MLB	26	0.75	0.00	5.56	0.0	98.0	44.2	13	41.3
2020	SEA	MLB	27	1.60	5.89	5.66	-0.1	97.5	44.7	13.1	41.8

Seattle Mariners 2020

LINEOUTS

Hitters

HITTER	POS	TEAM	LVL	AGE	PA	R	2B	3B	HR	RBI	BB	K	SB	CS	AVG/OBP/SLG	DRC+	WARP
Carter Bins	C	EVE	A-	20	202	31	2	0	7	26	33	56	5	2	.208/.391/.357	127	1.5
Braden Bishop	CF	MOD	A+	25	29	7	1	1	0	3	2	9	0	0	.240/.345/.360	56	0.2
	CF	SEA	MLB	25	60	3	0	0	0	4	3	21	0	0	.107/.153/.107	45	-0.2
	CF	TAC	AAA	25	211	29	15	0	8	31	23	44	2	2	.276/.360/.486	92	0.6
Tim Lopes	2B	SEA	MLB	25	128	11	7	0	1	12	15	29	6	3	.270/.359/.360	91	0.2
	2B	TAC	AAA	25	420	59	31	2	10	60	36	72	26	9	.302/.362/.476	99	0.9
Dylan Moore	UT	TAC	AAA	26	35	3	0	0	0	7	3	3	2	1	.172/.294/.172	49	-0.1
	UT	SEA	MLB	26	282	31	14	2	9	28	25	93	11	9	.206/.302/.389	79	0.4
Brian O'Keefe	C	SFD	AA	25	346	36	9	0	13	40	37	71	1	1	.229/.319/.389	82	0.6
Dom Thompson-Williams	OF	ARK	AA	24	479	46	24	4	12	41	35	152	15	2	.234/.298/.391	100	0.8
Patrick Wisdom	3B	TEX	MLB	27	28	1	1	0	0	1	1	15	0	0	.154/.185/.192	48	-0.2
	3B	NAS	AAA	27	453	68	15	0	31	74	53	125	8	2	.240/.332/.513	111	2.0

A reputation as an elite defensive catcher at Fresno State had some evaluators thinking **Carter Bins** could go early on Day 2 of the Draft. *Narrator*: He did not. Seattle scooped him up for $350K in the 11th round. ⓧ **Braden Bishop** suffered a lacerated spleen when he was hit by a pitch, threatening his health and derailing his season. His premier glove in center should secure him a bench spot in the majors when healthy. ⓧ If not for a brief study abroad experience with Toronto, **Tim Lopes**, Seattle's sixth-round selection in the 2012 Draft, would be the longest-tenured member of the Mariners organization this side of Kyle Seager. He'll enter 2020 just 376 home runs behind Jeff Kent on the all-time Edison High School alumni MLB home run list. ⓧ Could the Mariners have hit big in the international market for the second year in a row? Teenage shortstop **Noelvi Marte** followed up Julio Rodriguez's 2018 DSL MVP campaign with an MVP season of his own, thanks to a hot finish, posting a 1.221 OPS in his final 20 games. ⓧ **Dylan Moore** made at least one start at every position on the diamond other than pitcher and catcher, and he did manage to make some appearances on the mound. Impressive work for a player generated 15 seasons into your MLB: The Show franchise mode. ⓧ Either the Mariners selected **Brian O'Keefe** in the minor-league portion of the Rule 5 draft due to his offensive competency, or they confused him with the *Fortune* editor of the same name. We'd guess the former, but maybe Dipoto is cracking down on that "DiPoto" business. ⓧ Sharp home/road splits in favor of away games suggest **Dom Thompson-Williams** was another victim of the cavernous home park in Arkansas, but it's unclear if he did enough to avoid being sent back to Little Rock in 2020. ⓧ Despite his surname, **Patrick Wisdom** hasn't proven smart enough to avoid striking out in 40 percent of his career plate appearances. As such, he's exactly the type of Quad-A talent Jerry Dipoto swears he can stop collecting at any time, no really, he's in total control.

Seattle Mariners 2020

Pitchers

PITCHER	TEAM	LVL	AGE	W	L	SV	G	GS	IP	H	HR	BB/9	K/9	K	GB%	WHIP	ERA	DRA	WARP
Elvis Alvarado	NAT	Rk	20	2	2	0	7	2	15	10	0	9.6	11.4	19	51%	1.73	6.00	5.59	0.0
	MRN	Rk	20	0	1	0	5	1	12	10	0	2.2	9.8	13	29%	1.08	2.25	2.75	0.4
Chasen Bradford	SEA	MLB	29	0	0	1	12	0	16^2	17	6	2.2	5.9	11	52%	1.26	4.86	5.16	0.0
Matt Carasiti	TAC	AAA	27	1	0	4	15	0	16^1	19	3	3.9	9.4	17	45%	1.59	4.96	5.21	0.2
	IOW	AAA	27	1	1	1	16	0	27	20	1	3.7	7.7	23	55%	1.15	2.67	4.48	0.5
	SEA	MLB	27	0	1	0	11	5	9^2	11	2	4.7	9.3	10	50%	1.66	4.66	4.36	0.1
Nabil Crismatt	ARK	AA	24	4	5	0	14	13	83^2	57	6	1.2	9.6	89	44%	0.81	1.94	2.70	2.3
	TAC	AAA	24	0	5	0	13	8	46^2	67	15	4.1	13.1	68	37%	1.89	9.06	7.33	-0.3
Sam Delaplane	MOD	A+	24	3	2	2	21	0	31^2	22	2	4.0	17.6	62	40%	1.14	4.26	3.03	0.6
	ARK	AA	24	3	1	5	25	0	37	13	2	2.2	14.1	58	39%	0.59	0.49	1.60	1.4
Matt Festa	TAC	AAA	26	1	1	5	23	0	30^2	23	3	4.1	9.7	33	36%	1.21	2.64	2.81	1.0
	SEA	MLB	26	0	2	0	20	0	22^1	20	5	4.8	8.5	21	40%	1.43	5.64	5.57	-0.1
Aaron Fletcher	HAG	A	23	2	3	1	15	0	28	14	0	1.6	9.0	28	44%	0.68	1.61	2.45	0.8
	POT	A+	23	3	1	0	12	0	26	15	1	2.8	11.1	32	56%	0.88	1.38	2.83	0.6
	ARK	AA	23	0	0	0	9	0	13	14	0	2.1	10.4	15	54%	1.31	3.46	5.57	-0.2
	HAR	AA	23	0	0	0	5	0	6^1	7	0	2.8	12.8	9	62%	1.42	4.26	4.67	0.0
Joey Gerber	MOD	A+	22	0	2	8	25	0	26	17	0	4.2	13.5	39	39%	1.12	3.46	2.41	0.7
	ARK	AA	22	1	2	0	19	0	22^2	21	2	2.8	11.9	30	41%	1.24	1.59	4.30	0.1
Wyatt Mills	ARK	AA	24	4	2	8	41	0	52^2	43	2	2.9	11.3	66	55%	1.14	4.27	4.29	0.2
Anthony Misiewicz	ARK	AA	24	1	2	0	7	7	35^2	36	0	1.8	9.1	36	51%	1.21	2.52	4.45	0.2
	TAC	AAA	24	8	6	0	19	17	95^2	95	17	2.6	8.4	89	44%	1.29	5.36	3.83	2.6
Andrew Moore	ARK	AA	25	2	1	0	5	5	28	24	1	1.3	9.3	29	33%	1.00	3.86	3.34	0.6
	TAC	AAA	25	0	5	0	13	8	54	71	14	2.8	6.0	36	38%	1.63	8.00	6.49	0.0
	DUR	AAA	25	0	2	0	5	4	17^1	29	9	5.2	5.2	10	32%	2.25	12.98	8.94	-0.4
	SEA	MLB	25	0	0	0	1	1	4^2	6	2	1.9	3.9	2	18%	1.50	7.71	8.25	-0.1
Penn Murfee	MOD	A+	25	5	5	0	26	20	102^2	95	3	2.0	10.7	122	49%	1.15	3.07	3.93	1.3
	TAC	AAA	25	0	0	0	5	0	8^2	13	3	7.3	12.5	12	48%	2.31	10.38	6.80	0.0
Ljay Newsome	MOD	A+	22	6	6	0	18	18	100^2	105	11	0.8	11.1	124	27%	1.13	3.75	4.26	0.9
	ARK	AA	22	3	4	0	9	9	48^2	41	4	1.3	6.5	35	37%	0.99	2.77	4.08	0.5
Yohan Ramirez	BCA	A+	24	1	2	0	10	7	43^2	22	0	4.5	14.2	69	55%	1.01	2.89	2.73	1.2
	CCH	AA	24	3	5	1	17	8	62^1	42	5	7.5	12.9	89	45%	1.51	4.76	4.75	0.0
Connor Sadzeck	SEA	MLB	27	0	1	1	20	0	23^2	18	3	5.7	10.3	27	46%	1.39	2.66	4.36	0.3
Ricardo Sanchez	ARK	AA	22	8	12	0	27	27	146	157	10	2.3	8.3	135	51%	1.34	4.44	5.66	-1.2

PITCHER	TEAM	LVL	AGE	W	L	SV	G	GS	IP	H	HR	BB/9	K/9	K	GB%	WHIP	ERA	DRA	WARP
Phillip Valdez	NAS	AAA	27	1	7	1	26	14	78²	87	10	4.1	7.4	65	53%	1.56	4.92	4.70	1.4
	TEX	MLB	27	0	0	0	11	0	16	17	3	5.1	10.1	18	54%	1.62	3.94	4.54	0.1
Arodys Vizcaino	ATL	MLB	28	1	0	1	4	0	4	3	1	6.8	13.5	6	25%	1.50	2.25	5.04	0.0
Brandon Williamson	EVE	A-	21	0	0	0	10	9	15¹	9	0	2.9	14.7	25	55%	0.91	2.35	2.25	0.5

Elvis Alvarado is a converted outfielder with premium velocity, the kind of quintessential low-level lottery ticket you tack onto a last-minute July deal, which is exactly what Seattle did when they acquired him from Washington minutes before the deadline. ⓧ A frequent perplexer in everyone's favorite trivia game, "Country Music Star or Relief Pitcher?" **Chasen Bradford** spent much of the season on the injured list before succumbing to Tommy John Surgery, which will keep him out of action until late 2020. More time to work on those songs. ⓧ After a long college season as the ace for Arkansas, **Isaiah Campbell** didn't throw a professional pitch after signing. If he climbs the ladder successfully, he could become the first Portuguese-born major leaguer since Frank Thompson debuted for the Brooklyn Atlantics. ⓧ In a bullpen chock full of anonymous 20-something-year-old right-handers named Matt, **Matt Carasiti** was the most anonymous of them all. Having spent 2018 in Japan, he returned to affiliated ball briefly with the Cubs before Seattle scooped him up in June. ⓧ The Mariners inked **Kristian Cardozo**, a Venezuelan right-hander, for a reported $595,000 bonus in July. He's shown the ability to hit the low 90s with his fastball and also shows a breaking ball and a changeup. ⓧ 2017 second-rounder **Sam Carlson** will look to improve upon his current career average of one inning pitched per season. Reports out of Peoria indicate that Carlson's fastball velocity has returned, and he should finally see the jump to A-ball this year. ⓧ There are only two A's in the name **Nabil Crismatt**, which may explain why he continues to dominate Double-A (2.82 ERA in 195 career Double-A innings) and get absolutely rocked in Triple-A (8.96 ERA in 85.1 career Triple-A innings). ⓧ No relief pitcher with at least 50 innings across the minors posted a higher strikeout rate than **Sam Delaplane**, who politely sat down 45.8 percent of the batters he faced across two levels; not bad for a 23rd-round senior sign. ⓧ It was a confounding year for reliever **Matt Festa**, who was good enough to make the Opening Day roster but apparently not valued enough to warrant a September call-up. He bounced between Tacoma and Seattle seven (!) times in the interim. ⓧ A big element of success is being in the right place at the right time. Meanwhile, **Aaron Fletcher** is a fastball/slider lefty in a league that just eliminated the LOOGY. The fastball has some bite to it, which is his inside straight draw for making it to the major leagues. ⓧ **Joey Gerber**'s streak of having never started a game in college or the pros will surely be broken whenever he is first asked to be an opener, a role that could fit his arsenal quite nicely. ⓧ It was another stellar statistical season for side-arming slinger **Wyatt Mills**. The Gonzaga product and

Seattle Mariners 2020

Spokane native should spend much of 2020 back in the Evergreen State, whether it be in Tacoma or Seattle. ⚾ We're still waiting to find out what was so special about left-hander **Anthony Misiewicz** that the Mariners re-acquired him from the Rays just 16 months after trading him there in the first place. ⚾ It took less than a year for **Andrew Moore** to boomerang back to the organization that drafted him after being traded to Tampa Bay in 2018. He'll resume his lifelong quest to prove that crafty right-handers can be major leaguers too. ⚾ Penn Badgley is the guy in *Gossip Girl* and *Easy A*, Penn Jillette is the loud part of *Penn & Teller* and **Penn Murfee** is a 25-year-old who raced to Triple-A last year. The word on Murfee is that deception is part of the low-slot hurler's game and his breaking ball is an easy above-average offering, but turning a 33rd-rounder into a major leaguer? That's magic. ⚾ With peripherals that outpace his pure stuff, **Ljay Newsome** appears to have taken the organizational motto "Control the Zone" to heart. The right-hander posted a microscopic, MiLB-best 2.7 walk rate in 155 innings while striking out more than a batter per inning for the first time in his career. ⚾ A big dude with a big fastball. There's a lot to dream about, but an inconsistent delivery and below-average off-speed stuff have kept **Yohan Ramirez** from reaching his full potential. ⚾ Built like a small-ball power forward, the gigantic **Connor Sadzeck** is still chucking high-90s cheese with a vicious slider, but his continued inability to stay in the strike zone or on the field probably made it easier for Texas to ship him to the division rival M's. He got his second Tommy John surgery in October. ⚾ Once a prized teenage left-hander with mid-rotation upside, **Ricardo Sánchez** still has big league promise—he's just lost some luster. ⚾ **Phillips Valdez** followed in the footsteps of Austin Bibens-Dirkx and Brandon Mann to make his big-league debut with the Rangers after many years in the minors. He was good, but apparently not quite good enough to keep on the 40-man roster; the Mariners got him on a waiver claim not long after the end of the season. ⚾ **Arodys Vizcaíno**'s season was already over due to shoulder surgery when he was acquired by Seattle for salary purposes, so it's quite possible his tenure with the Mariners never even featured a single trip to T-Mobile Park. He'll either eventually return fully equipped with his tantalizing stuff, or he'll become the next electric arm to fall victim to its own nastiness, a sparkling blip in the long history of short-lived dynamite relievers. ⚾ "Welcome to the Big Leagues" could be a headline you see one day about 2019 second-round pick **Brandon Williamson**, a hard-throwing left-hander who grew up in the small rural town of Welcome, Minnesota.

Mariners Prospects

The State of the System

The…Mariners system…is good?

The Top Ten

1. ★ ★ ★ 2020 Top 101 Prospect #7 ★ ★ ★

Jarred Kelenic OF OFP: 70 ETA: 2020-21
Born: 07/16/99 Age: 20 Bats: L Throws: L Height: 6'0" Weight: 196
Origin: Round 1, 2018 Draft (#6 overall)

The Report: Mets fans, don't read this…

Mariners fans, hello.

Kelenic's stock started shooting up early in the season when he showed off an improved swing path while dominating the Low-A South Atlantic League. He was promoted to High-A shortly after Memorial Day and performed quite well. He was promoted again to Double-A less than a month after his 20th birthday for the August stretch run and Texas League playoffs, and he kept hitting against upper-minors pitching too. So much for the draft-time concerns about being on the older side for a prep bat.

Kelenic has a chance to be a five-tool player. Not one of those dudes who has a bunch of 5s and a 55 run who occasionally gets called a five-tool player, but an actual five-tool star that collects black ink and awards. He projects for plus hit and plus power from a sweet, classic lefty swing. He's a present plus runner with a plus arm. The weakest projection at the moment is defensive. The routes and closing ability aren't quite there for a sure-shot bet in center yet, and we could easily see a team preferring him in a corner, especially if he slows down as he moves through his 20s. But it's not out of the question that he ends up as a net positive in center down the road.

Variance: Medium. Our degree of confidence that he ends up as a good regular is high, but the positional risk that he'll slide to a corner is significant, and that would put a lot of pressure on the bat. Getting to a 70 OFP as a corner outfielder means you have to hit.

Mark Barry's Fantasy Take: Quibble about the order of the top two here if you'd like, but for now, in the year of the pig, Kelenic gets the narrow nod mostly thanks to proximity. It's not just because of the timetable, though. Kelenic snagged 20 bags in 2019 in addition to hitting for power and average. That, as they say, is very good. If Kelenic isn't a top-10 dynasty guy right now, he's definitely beating down the doors. I'm really sorry, Mets fans, but at least you'll always have the Edwin Díaz memories to fall back on.

───────── ★ ★ ★ *2020 Top 101 Prospect* **#10** ★ ★ ★ ─────────

2 Julio Rodriguez OF   OFP: 70   ETA: 2021
Born: 12/29/00   Age: 19   Bats: R   Throws: R   Height: 6'4"   Weight: 225
Origin: International Free Agent, 2017

The Report: Signed by the Mariners in July of 2017, Rodriguez has one of the higher-end offensive packages in all of the minors. Just 18 years old during his first full season in the states, he showed an extremely advanced approach at the plate. He controls the zone well and routinely finds his pitch to hit. His swing is compact, quick and showcases an ability to hit line-to-line. Rodriguez hit 12 homers in 84 games this year, but he has yet to fully tap into his power stroke. Once he matures, 25-plus home runs will not be out of the question.

Rodriguez is sneaky fast on the basepaths. He isn't a burner but displays the wheels to be a slightly above-average stolen base threat. In early looks defensively he looked like an average fielder at best. But on second inspection he has the potential to play a slightly above-average center field. Additionally, his plus arm can play anywhere on the grass.

Variance: Medium. Rodriguez is still very young and has not played a full slate of games yet, with that comes a little uncertainty. Also uncertain is his ability to tap into his power tool as he grows. That will be the key to him reaching his full potential.

Mark Barry's Fantasy Take: The second part of a one-two punch rarely seen outside of time-traveling bro duos from the 80s and 90s, Rodriguez offers one of the highest ceilings in the minor leagues, laying waste to two levels in 2019 before turning 19 years old. I kinda love this guy. If you want to go crazy and dream on .300/35/10, you're not going to get much pushback from me.

───────── ★ ★ ★ *2020 Top 101 Prospect* **#39** ★ ★ ★ ─────────

3 Logan Gilbert RHP   OFP: 60   ETA: 2021-22
Born: 05/05/97   Age: 23   Bats: R   Throws: R   Height: 6'6"   Weight: 225
Origin: Round 1, 2018 Draft (#14 overall)

The Report: Drafted in the first round in 2018, Gilbert dominated across three levels in his first pro season in 2019. The first thing that stands out when watching Gilbert is his confidence and mound presence–both resembling that of a seasoned vet. He backed it up with a solid four-pitch mix. The Stetson product's fastball sits in the low 90s but can touch 95 when needed. It's a straight pitch that plays up due to his command and extension. Gilbert's best secondary is a 12-6, mid-70s curveball that features late bite. This pitch is a plus swing-and-miss offering, whether he throws it in the zone or buries it in the dirt. His third pitch is a slider that sits 80-82 mph. It doesn't have hard bite but shows slightly above-average sweeping action. Gilbert added a mid-80s changeup this year which dives out of the zone with some fade and he seems to have a decent feel for it. Gilbert is able to mix and command all four offerings, attacking the zone without fear and with an understanding of how to sequence his arsenal.

Variance: Medium. With sound mechanics, an ability to consistently throw strikes and a solid four-pitch mix, Gilbert has set himself a fairly high floor.

Mark Barry's Fantasy Take: I'm of two minds with Gilbert. I, like our venerable leader, Bret Sayre, mentioned last year, have a hard time trusting super tall guys to repeat their mechanics enough to be effective for the duration of an outing. There are just a lot of moving parts to account for. That said, Gilbert just barely crept above a 1.00 WHIP during his time in Modesto, and stayed below that benchmark in his two other stops—maybe it's much ado about nothing. I'd like his slider and changeup to garner a few more whiffs, but I'd also like Manny Machado money to write these comments, so I guess the lesson is we can't always get what we want. Gilbert has SP3 upside, but will probably settle in as a SP5-6.

★ ★ ★ *2020 Top 101 Prospect* **#62** ★ ★ ★

4

Evan White   1B   OFP: 55   ETA: Late 2020
Born: 04/26/96   Age: 24   Bats: R   Throws: L   Height: 6'3"   Weight: 205
Origin: Round 1, 2017 Draft (#17 overall)

The Report: White carried his late 2018 power surge over into 2019, setting a career high for home runs in just over half a season. He's filled out with good weight since college and added enough loft to his swing to project at least average game power. He hasn't added much in the way of length to his stroke, and it remains a compact swing with above-average bat speed. White's hit tool and glove have never been concerns. He will likely have seasons where he hits .300, and it's an easy plus projection otherwise. His defense at first is gold glove caliber. While there was talk of his playing the outfield off and on over his pro career, he's been first-base-only, but not with the pessimistic connotation that usually carries. It's an unusual first base profile—the bats-right-throws-left thing is still truly bizarre—but the bat is good enough now that it's a fairly safe one.

Variance: Medium. White is a weird profile at first base—there were thoughts he could handle center—and he's been a slow burn of marginal improvement or consolidation year-over-year. That makes him already 23 and only in Double-A, but the developments have all been positive. There's somewhat limited upside here, but if the power gains in Double-A continue to carry over, there's no reason he can't be a plus regular. We just need to see it for a bit longer.

Mark Barry's Fantasy Take: I've heard Cody Bellinger and Paul Goldschmidt fantasy comps for White, and I think if you expect anything approaching that level of production, you'll be sorely disappointed. There's a chance he could be good-Eric Hosmer, though, which is not that bad, if a touch less sparkly.

5. Justin Dunn   RHP

OFP: 55   ETA: 2019
Born: 09/22/95   Age: 24   Bats: R   Throws: R   Height: 6'2"   Weight: 185
Origin: Round 1, 2016 Draft (#19 overall)

The Report: The shape of Dunn's profile has changed fairly significantly from when he was drafted in the first round out of Boston College. He's bled a bit of fastball velocity and now sits more in the low 90s, touching 95, but he has developed a full complement of average-or-better secondaries. The fastball command is still fringy, but he's more consistently showing the kind of late arm-side run that he only flashed as a Mets prospect. The changeup development has been key here, as the pitch is now above-average despite less-than-ideal command and velocity separation. Dunn sells the pitch well and it has above-average tumble and fade. The mid-80s slider has been his best offspeed historically, and continues to be a potential plus pitch. It's sharp enough to backfoot to lefties, and Dunn commands the pitch well. He started working a curveball in more often in 2018 as a different breaking ball look. It's a useful addition to the arsenal, although more of a spot than chase pitch, and does bleed into the slider at times.

Dunn probably isn't actually 6-foot-2 and has gotten stockier, although he's still able to repeat an athletic delivery with good arm speed. In some ways there is a lot less reliever risk here than there was coming out of the draft, but he also doesn't have a late inning fallback anymore if the command isn't fine enough against major league hitters as a starter. However, he looks more like a rotation cog now than he has in years past, with the potential for four above-average offerings. His pitchability and confidence in the secondary stuff has improved as well. Dunn has different ways to beat you each time through the order now and looks like a major-league-ready mid-rotation starter.

Variance: Low. The Mariners tried to keep Dunn out of the PCL which led to him repeating Double-A as a 23-year-old, where he wasn't as dominant as you'd like. I don't read much into the wildness in his MLB cup of coffee, but if there is something that will undo him in the majors, it's the command and control profile, so that's worth monitoring. Overall though, the broad arsenal gives him a lot of options. Dunn could win a 2020 major league job out of camp.

Mark Barry's Fantasy Take: Dunn is sort of like plain toast. It's not the good stuff that you really want, but it's not bad either. I think he'll be better as a mid-rotation starter in real life than fantasy, but he could have some SP4-5 good years ahead. He'll be useful. I'm really sorry, Mets fans, but at least you'll always have the Edwin Díaz memories to fall back on.

6 **George Kirby   RHP**   OFP: 55   ETA: 2021
Born: 02/04/98   Age: 22   Bats: R   Throws: R   Height: 6'4"   Weight: 201
Origin: Round 1, 2019 Draft (#20 overall)

The Report: Lacking the typical "wow" stuff you find in first-round pitchers, what Kirby does have as a carrying tool is plus-plus command of a four-pitch repertoire. In the 2019 calendar year between starting games at Elon University and his professional debut for the Mariners in the Northwest League, Kirby walked just SIX batters in 111 1/3 innings while striking out 132 along the way. It's not just fastball command, either, as he is able to land each of his pitches for strikes while also making in-game adjustments when he knows a pitch is slightly off.

The fastball sits comfortably in the low 90s but there is enough arm strength to ramp into the mid 90s when he wants to reach back for it. It's used relentlessly the first time through the order, peppering every quadrant of the zone. In two-strike counts and the second time through both a curveball and slider can be deployed to get hitters off balance. There are also signs of a good changeup that could be an average-to-better pitch. The awareness of his abilities and body control are unteachable qualities and, with some room still left to fill out, Kirby could jump several levels in 2020.

Variance: Low. No history of injuries, a developed college pitcher, and the command/control ability that he can lean on throughout his career gives him a high floor, even if there is a limited ceiling.

Mark Barry's Fantasy Take: It's hard not to fall in love with Kirby's control. He's walked zero dudes in his professional career, which is equal parts awe-inspiring and hilarious. His fantasy usefulness will rest almost solely on his ability to strike guys out. Sometimes these extreme control guys yield Shane Bieber and sometimes they yield Josh Tomlin. I'd jump on Kirby in a 200ish prospect league hoping for the former, while ready to cut bait on the latter.

7 **Juan Then   RHP**   OFP: 60   ETA: 2022
Born: 02/07/00   Age: 20   Bats: R   Throws: R   Height: 6'1"   Weight: 155
Origin: International Free Agent, 2016

The Report: Then has taken a more circuitous route to full-season baseball than most of his West Virginia Power teammates. He was traded from the Mariners to the Yankees before coming stateside, and then back to the Mariners in exchange for Edwin Encarnacion last summer. After the return trade, and a few weeks in rookie ball, he made his full-season debut in mid-August of this year. You'll undoubtedly hear more about those deals in the future, and Then's route will be offered as a microcosm of Jerry Dipoto's tenure in Seattle.

But let's talk about Then the prospect, and he's developed into a good one. He has a thin, athletic frame with narrow hips, which means he should always be on the slight side. He fields his position well and looks cat-like coming off the mound. At present the mechanics are a bit inconsistent, but he's athletic enough that those issues should be ironed out down the road. He has a very quick arm with a short path and topped out at 96 with sharp arm-side run in my look. All three pitches are above-average, but the curveball will likely be his best offering when it's all said and done. The change is a bit firm right now, but it's still advanced for his age. He should be able to throw all his pitches with confidence and get plenty of swing-and-miss both in the zone and out of it. Then's mound presence is something that could use some work—he looks anxious at times, but seems to benefit from mound visits and make adjustments in-game. Expect a bump in velocity as he gets stronger and adds mass to his lower half.

Variance: High. Then only has three full-season starts under his belt. He's athletic, but there are issues that need to be worked out. He's a small righty. Added strength will go a long way with Then, and he has all the right pieces to turn into solid piece in any big-league rotation.

Mark Barry's Fantasy Take: Then is an intriguing prospect, both for his work on the bump and the fun we could have with his surname in tweets. He's pretty young and far away, though. I wouldn't argue if you're the gambling sort and want to take a flier, but I probably wouldn't roster Then outside of the deepest, 350-plus prospect leagues.

8 Noelvi Marte SS   OFP: 60   ETA: 2024ish
Born: 10/16/01   Age: 18   Bats: R   Throws: R   Height: 6'1"   Weight: 181
Origin: International Free Agent, 2018

The Report: I had a discussion on our podcast Discord recently (Ed. Become a patron and join today!) about what counts as useful data when it comes to IFA guys with little or no stateside experience. Bonus numbers end up out of date fast. Sure, there were a few prospects in our Top 25 who were seven-figure bonus babies, but for every Wander Franco there's a Gilbert Lara. For every Vlad Jr., a Kevin Maitan. And there's five-figure bonus guys right behind them as well. The bonus figures might have been a decent approximation of talent at the time of agreeing to them, but things change quickly for teenage baseball players, and the deals aren't being magically agreed to on the morning of July 2nd anyway.

Complex-league stats are mostly useless—I honestly wish they didn't keep them—but how quickly a player gets assigned stateside might not be? Eh, I'm not convinced. I don't think Marte is necessarily a worse prospect solely because he spent the summer mashing in the Dominican instead of Peoria. Acculturation isn't just about adjusting to the level of competition stateside, so I don't particularly read anything into Marte being in the DSL while, say, Kevin Alcantara and Orelvis Martinez came stateside.

What that does mean though, is our staff has less info on Noelvi Marte. So he falls more into the Jasson Dominguez or Robert Puason bucket than the Marco Luciano one. But we don't have any reason to think he isn't still a potential plus shortstop so…

Variance: Extreme.

Mark Barry's Fantasy Take: Ah, a teenager who dominated the DSL, flashing power, speed and average—what could possibly go wrong? Age and proximity aside, Marte is a hot name in the fantasy community right now, so you're going to have to take the plunge early if you want any shares. If Marte hits in Everett like he did in 2019, people will lose their damn minds and he'll be untouchable. Get in early, whether you want to or not.

9 — Justus Sheffield   LHP   OFP: 55   ETA: 2018
Born: 05/13/96   Age: 24   Bats: L   Throws: L   Height: 6'0"   Weight: 200
Origin: Round 1, 2014 Draft (#31 overall)

The Report: Sheffield had a nice run of three straight years in the 50s on the 101, which was the inspiration for me to write his prospect blurb as Alanis Morissette song verse in last year's Annual, as if a child of the 90s needs such inspiration. He will, uh, not be in the 50-59 band of this year's 101. Even including caveats about the ball, he looked so bad in Triple-A that he was sent back to Double-A in June. He pitched well enough after the demotion to earn another September call-up, but he should have given that he originally mastered the level in 2017.

This is Sheffield's sixth eligible list cycle (for context, the first BP top ten he was on was headlined by Francisco Lindor). Suffice to say, we have a lot of priors and comfort with him as a staff. He most typically works 92-94 as a starter, touching 96, and he's shown a bit higher out of the bullpen in the past. The slider is the potential out pitch here, a tight mid-80s offering that he threw over 35 percent of the time in the majors in 2019. He also mixes in a changeup that has flashed but still lacks consistency. His command has come and gone for most of his pro career, and continued to be evasive in 2019. While he pitched a nice combined 169 innings last season, he's had durability questions linger for most of his prospectdom, and he's still short.

We've tipped for years because of all this that Sheffield's future might be in the bullpen, and the needle certainly moved a bit further in that direction in 2019. At the same time, Seattle's not likely to be competitive anytime real soon, so they're likely to keep running Sheffield out there as a starter in the fading hopes that he can replicate James Paxton, the pitcher he was most recently traded for.

Variance: High. As noted, he's been a 60 OFP and a 101 guy for us with some regularity recently, and the arm talent is certainly still there. We're just giving him a lower chance to reach the higher outcomes in his band because he stalled out this year, basically.

Mark Barry's Fantasy Take: Boy, was that a 2019 season for Sheffield, huh? I haven't seen a lefty with such promise suffer that kind of fall from grace since, well, nevermind. Sheffield should still be useful in AL-only leagues or deep-mixed formats, but it's hard to imagine he'll ever reach that SP2 upside and might be relegated to a back-of-the-rotation guy.

10 Jake Fraley   OF   OFP: 55   ETA: 2019
Born: 05/25/95   Age: 25   Bats: L   Throws: L   Height: 6'0"   Weight: 195
Origin: Round 2, 2016 Draft (#77 overall)

The Report: Before 2019, Fraley was generally regarded as a toolsy bat with potential, but his issues staying on the field left him a bit lost in the shuffle in a very deep Rays system. He found a new home in Seattle via one of Dipoto's fourteen-hundred trades and promptly put together a breakout season in his new organization. Fraley is a plus athlete with plus, whippy, bat speed and the ability to find the barrel in every quadrant of the zone. He certainly enjoyed his brief time mashing the Triple-A ball, but the overall game power projection is more average than plus. He can also have issues with spin, which is something that got exposed in his first taste of major league action.

In the field—despite above-average speed—Fraley is best-suited to a corner, and likely left field due to fringe arm strength, although he can cover center for you. The profile can look a bit tweenerish at times, but we think there is enough bat and baserunning here to give Fraley a decent shot at being an everyday player somewhere on the outfield grass.

Variance: Medium. Fraley has conquered the upper minors, but there's a track record of durability issues and still lingering questions about the hit tool against major league offspeed stuff.

Mark Barry's Fantasy Take: Fraley might be a rare case of "better in fantasy than real life." He offers a little power, a little speed and he should see plenty of playing time this season in Seattle. The upside might be limited, but he could be an OF4 as soon as 2020 in standard formats (OBP leagues might be rough because Fraley literally didn't walk once in a 12-game cup of coffee in September).

The Next Ten

11 Kyle Lewis   OF
Born: 07/13/95   Age: 24   Bats: R   Throws: R   Height: 6'4"   Weight: 210
Origin: Round 1, 2016 Draft (#11 overall)

Lewis's power surge in the majors in September was a great story. After a catastrophic knee injury during his pro debut back in 2016 it wasn't clear if he'd make it at all, let alone have a run like that. While he hit the ball incredibly hard across 75 major-league plate appearances, the overall profile hasn't changed all that much, and the September run frankly looks like a bit of an outlier given that he slugged under .400 in Double-A. There's plus raw and an uppercut conducive to power here, but the swing requires a lot of effort to unlock that pop and the approach isn't great. Those factors led to a 38.7 percent strikeout rate in the majors, after he struck out 29.3 percent of the time in Double-A. The knee injury sapped his speed, and he's best suited to a corner now. There might be enough boom in the profile to carry the offensive burden of a corner spot, and his OFP is the same as Evan White's up at number four in the system. We just see higher risk here given the swing-and-miss and overall approach issues.

12 Cal Raleigh C
Born: 11/26/96   Age: 23   Bats: B   Throws: R   Height: 6'3"   Weight: 215
Origin: Round 3, 2018 Draft (#90 overall)

The Mariners have a lot of potential above-average bats in the organization now, and Raleigh rounds out that tier. You could argue for him several spots higher as he's perhaps the best bet to play in the majors for a while given the positive developments behind the plate and with the bat. It's a pretty traditional stocky catcher's frame, but he shows solid athleticism both in receiving and blocking, and his receiving has improved to the point where he's a good bet to be at least an average glove. While his arm isn't the strongest, he will at least keep would-be base stealers honest.

Raleigh has flashed plus raw from both sides of the plate and brought that pop into games this year. Yes, most of that season was spent as an advanced college bat in the Cal League, but regardless, there's the potential for 20-homer power in the majors. He has above-average bat speed although the swing can get a bit mechanical at times. The hit tool might end up a bit fringy, but he's a true two-way catching prospect now, and a strong Double-A campaign could fire him up this list next year and onto national radars.

13 Brandon Williamson LHP
Born: 04/02/98   Age: 22   Bats: L   Throws: L   Height: 6'6"   Weight: 210
Origin: Round 2, 2019 Draft (#59 overall)

A big lefty who signed underslot as a second-round pick out of TCU, Williamson offers an intriguing combination of the present and the projectable. Not as dominant his junior year as you'd expect given the size and stuff, Williamson showed off a four-pitch arsenal as a pro that overwhelmed Northwest League hitters. The fastball is low 90s, but his height and high-three-quarters slot makes it a tough angle for batters. He showed two different breaking ball looks: a slider he could bury to get chases and a big breaking curve to spot. Both are potentially average offerings. The change is the fourth pitch and will need to develop to keep him on pace for a back-of-the-rotation destination, but the size and delivery look

Seattle Mariners 2020

the part of an innings eater. It's a lean body so you could dream on him adding some strength and velocity, but Williamson's frame is on the narrow side, so I don't know how much more fastball you are actually going to wring out here.

14 Isaiah Campbell   RHP
Born: 08/15/97   Age: 22   Bats: R   Throws: R   Height: 6'4"   Weight: 225
Origin: Round 2, 2019 Draft (#76 overall)

Campbell was one of the better college arms available—granted not a banner year for that cohort—so the Mariners were likely thrilled he slipped to their Comp B pick. He's a big, physically mature righty who features a potentially above-average fastball/slider combo. The fastball has some plane from a high-three-quarters slot and can touch 95, while the slider at its best is a mid-80s hard breaker with good shape and depth. There's better feel for a changeup than you'd expect, but it's not so advanced that there isn't a fair bit of reliever risk here. But whatever role he makes the majors in, when he does he will be the first Portuguese-born major leaguer since Frank Thompson who played for the 1875 incarnation of the Washington Nationals. Campbell pitched deep into the summer with the Razorbacks; the Mariners kept him off short-season mounds and throwing sim games for the balance of 2019, so we will have to wait and see how he adjusts to pro ball.

15 Sam Carlson   RHP
Born: 12/03/98   Age: 21   Bats: R   Throws: R   Height: 6'4"   Weight: 195
Origin: Round 2, 2017 Draft (#55 overall)

One of my least-favorite types of dart throws during list season is the "prospect arm who has missed significant time due to Tommy John surgery before throwing significant pro innings." Carlson threw…uh…/checks notes…three innings in 2017. Some of this is just the vagaries of timing. Carlson had his surgery in the summer of 2018 while in extended. So there's nothing unusual about his recovery so far. That all said, we won't have any real, actionable information about where to rank him until he steps back on a professional mound next year. What we do know is he was an OFP 55 for us coming out of the draft based on the projectability and present fastball/slider combo. So if that's all in its proper place in April, there's an argument he should be up with Dunn and Kirby. But the variance here is extreme, and until we see it, we are going to be cautious.

16 Ljay Newsome   RHP
Born: 11/08/96   Age: 23   Bats: R   Throws: R   Height: 5'11"   Weight: 210
Origin: Round 26, 2015 Draft (#785 overall)

Newsome always had plus command and major-league-quality secondaries, but even in the recent era of much shallower Mariners systems, it was tough to get on board with ranking a dude sitting in the mid-to-upper 80s with his fastball. But his velocity "spike" in 2019 has taken the profile from undesirable to undeniable. Well undeniably a back-end starter prospect, but hey, that's something. Newsome now sits around 90 and touches as high as 94. There's not much life on it, but he commands it well down in the zone. He'll have to. Now that he can at least establish the heater, the above-average slider and change play up. The secondaries were far too much for Cal League hitters, and got enough swings and misses against upper minors ones to portend good—or at least average—things in the majors. Newsome throws a lot of strikes, and the fastball is still below-average for a right-hander. It remains to be seen if he can live in the zone with this arsenal against major league bats. The Mariners seem unsure as they left him off the 40-man and unprotected in the Rule 5 draft, but given the improved fastball and how close to the majors he is now, he makes our list.

17 Braden Bishop   OF
Born: 08/22/93   Age: 26   Bats: R   Throws: R   Height: 6'1"   Weight: 190
Origin: Round 3, 2015 Draft (#94 overall)

Bishop has suffered through pretty bad injury luck the last two seasons. His 2018 was cut short by a broken forearm, and he missed a chunk of time this year with a lacerated spleen, the result of a hit by pitch. When on the field, though, he has remained indubitably Braden Bishop. He struggled badly across intermittent playing time with the big club, but hit in Triple-A and made good use of the new baseballs. Even when the bat isn't performing Bishop is a quality defender at all three outfield spots, so if he does manage to hit even a little bit he should have a long career as a bench outfielder.

18 Art Warren   RHP
Born: 03/23/93   Age: 27   Bats: R   Throws: R   Height: 6'3"   Weight: 230
Origin: Round 23, 2015 Draft (#695 overall)

After another season missing plenty of bats in Arkansas, Warren got his first cup of coffee in the majors. His brief success in September followed the same formula that has made him an intriguing relief prospect the past couple years. He throws a plus—flashing plus-plus—slider a lot. It's the very model of a modern major pen arm. The slider sits mid 80s with big downward bite. When on, it's basically unhittable. The slide piece can show a little bit more like a power slurve at times, which is the only thing keeping it from a straight 7 on our sheets. There's plenty of fastball, as well, as Warren sits 95 and touches higher. Even the good systems still have their 95-and-a-slider guys, but Warren's slider is good enough to play in the eighth or ninth.

19 Joey Gerber   RHP
Born: 05/03/97   Age: 23   Bats: R   Throws: R   Height: 6'4"   Weight: 215
Origin: Round 8, 2018 Draft (#238 overall)

Seattle Mariners 2020

When you go twenty deep on systems you start to realize that even the better systems tend to thin out in similar ways. So we've reached the reliever-only section of the Mariners list. Gerber is an eighth-round college closer made good, as his mid-90s fastball and mid-80s slider have dominated at every stop so far on Seattle's organizational ladder. You see the fastball pretty late out of the hand and the slider has hard, late tilt. Gerber has a violent delivery and below-average command of both his pitches, but the stuff is setup man quality.

20 **Damon Casetta-Stubbs   RHP**
Born: 07/22/99   Age: 20   Bats: R   Throws: R   Height: 6'4"   Weight: 225
Origin: Round 11, 2018 Draft (#328 overall)

We had Casetta-Stubbs 11th last year out of the draft as an overslot prep. He's not that much worse of a prospect this time around, which points to a generally improved system, although he struggled mightily as a 19-year-old aggressively assigned to full-season ball. He was more low 90s than mid 90s for me in April, and the slider is miles ahead of the changeup at present even though both lack consistency. He showed useful command, and I intuitively liked him a little more than I should've. He's got projectability left and the variance on both sides for where he's going to be even two years from now is extremely high, but there's the outline of a useful starter or reliever here. In short, he's an interesting live arm.

Personal Cheeseball

PC **Wyatt Mills   RHP**
Born: 01/25/95   Age: 25   Bats: R   Throws: R   Height: 6'3"   Weight: 175
Origin: Round 3, 2017 Draft (#93 overall)

Mills has struggled some in Double-A, which is not an unusual spot for your typical mid-round college sidearmer to run aground. Mills has a fair bit more stuff than that genus, though. He has average fastball velocity, regularly hitting 94, although it takes a lot of effort to dial it up, and he lacks the finer command you associate with a polished sidewinder. The slider flashes short, late frisbee action in the mid 80s, but it can have inconsistent shape or back up some. Everything is a bit too hittable for Mills to sneak onto the back of the list this year with Warren and Gerber, but nothing says personal cheeseball here at BP like a low-slot dude throwing bullets.

Low Minors Sleeper

 **Austin Shenton   3B**
Born: 01/22/98   Age: 22   Bats: L   Throws: R   Height: 6'0"   Weight: 195
Origin: Round 5, 2019 Draft (#156 overall)

The Mariners' fifth-round pick this year, Shenton offers a bit more projection than you usually find in a Day Two college bat. He isn't raw, either, taking to pro ball immediately and showing a viable hit tool. Shenton is short to the ball, with enough physical strength and bat speed to drive it. He's started to tap into some raw power as well, and he will need to continue to do so, as he's only passable at third, and might end up seeing time at first or an outfield corner. He could add further strength and power, allowing the bat to carry whatever defensive spot he mans. Shenton is worth keeping an eye on in full-season ball for sure.

Top Talents 25 and Under (as of 4/1/2020)

1. Jarred Kelenic
2. Julio Rodriguez
3. J.P. Crawford
4. Logan Gilbert
5. Evan White
6. Justin Dunn
7. George Kirby
8. Juan Then
9. Noelvi Marte
10. Justus Sheffield

The primary difference between art and sport is that sports have a predefined goal, a victory condition. Sports have one expression. The Seattle Mariners, therefore, are art.

The defining characteristic of this 25U isn't that it's good or bad—it's both good, and bad—but that it's nearly identical to the prospect list up top. Only Crawford is guaranteed a job in the majors this season, while Sheffield and Dunn may be pressed into service not out of merit but because of the contractual obligations of fielding a full roster. Not that it matters. Those games will have happened, technically, but they won't really happen. The 2020 Seattle Mariners won't really exist.

Come October, we'll agree that they couldn't have, that it was all some collective fever dream, an Out of the Park simulation retconned into the box scores. It won't have made sense for so much effort, so many millions of dollars and billions of hours to be pooled into the creation of something so thoroughly pointless as the 2020 Seattle Mariners, a product of planned obsolescence. Did they really stand in line to file through the metal detectors to watch the lineup get dissected by Justin Verlander? Did they really cheer for a Clayton Richard slider that caught a batter napping and stranded runners on the corners? No. It's not possible.

Seattle Mariners 2020

Jerry Dipoto has planted his flag in 2021 as the point in which the Mariners officially resume their pursuit of winning baseball games. (It was actually mid-2020, but that was before Sheffield's fall from grace, so he'd probably prefer we all forget that.) So the real #1 to look out for in the city of Seattle isn't Crawford, or even the team's playoff drought, nine months younger than Julio Rodriguez. It's the cognitive dissonance that goes into producing, consuming, and particularly selling this cardboard facade of a baseball team, ready to topple at the first gust of wind. Sports may be about winning and losing, but the acceptance and the rationalization of sports is an artistic expression. The good news: if, as Orson Welles said, "the enemy of art is the absence of limitation," 2020 will provide Mariners fans with so much art.

Part 3: Featured Articles

The Baseball Is Juiced (Again)

Robert Arthur

This article originally appeared at Baseball Prospectus on April 5, 2019.

It started when the normally reliable Chris Sale got lit up for three homers by the Mariners in the Red Sox's season opener. It was part of a record number of taters that flew on Opening Day, as starters from Sale to Zack Greinke were taken deep by the handful. Then Christian Yelich hit a home run in each of his first four games, tying yet another MLB record, this one for consecutive games with a dinger to start a season.

It didn't take long for fans and players to begin whispering and tweeting about the baseballs being juiced again. It's early yet for us to come to any definitive conclusion about the 2019 season, but preliminary data shows that the baseball has returned to its aerodynamic peak. Whether that means this season will smash home run records like 2017 did remains to be seen.

Before home run explosion over the last few years, no one worried too much about the baseball's air resistance. While MLB and Rawlings (the company that manufactures the official baseballs) kept track of dozens of metrics to make sure that the ball was consistent from month to month, they didn't measure drag.

But drag is incredibly important in determining how likely a hitter is to knock one out of the park. As baseballs become more aerodynamic, they travel further given a certain initial velocity. A deep fly ball that might have been caught at the warning track can instead go into the first row of the stands. A three percent change in drag coefficient can work to add about five feet to a well-hit fly ball, which can in turn increase home runs league wide by an astounding 10-15 percent.

It's possible to measure the aerodynamics of the baseball using the pitch-tracking radars currently in place in each MLB ballpark. By calculating the loss of speed from when the pitch is released to when it crosses the plate, you can directly measure the drag coefficient on the baseball. I first wrote about the role of decreasing drag in boosting home runs in 2017, and MLB's commission of scientists and statisticians later confirmed that the more aerodynamic baseballs in use that year were largely to blame for the spike in home runs. The same commission rejected some alternate hypotheses, like rising temperatures and a league-wide boost in launch angle pushing more balls over the fence.

The current era has featured some large fluctuations in drag coefficient, leading to first an explosion in 2016 and 2017, and then a dialing back of homers last year. Curious about the record-breaking home run tallies in the last few days, I used the same methodology to measure the aerodynamics of the baseballs so far in 2019.

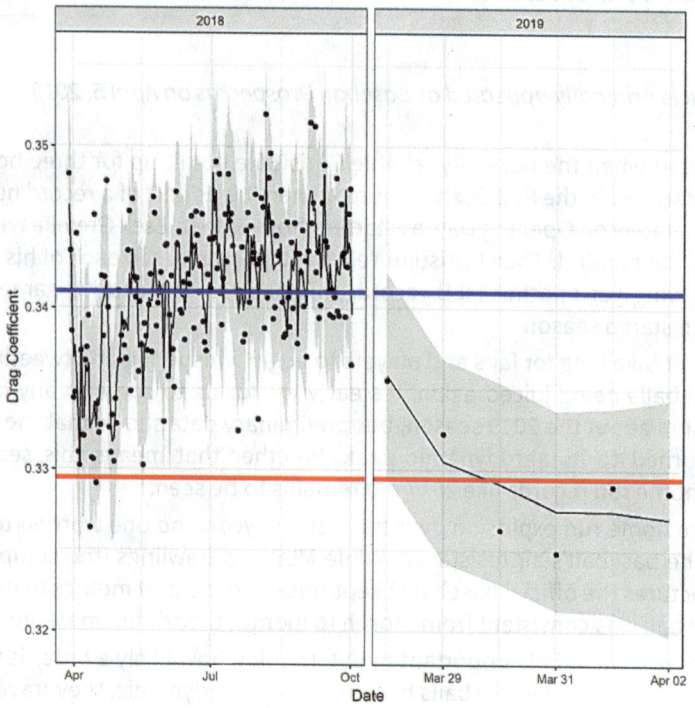

We're only a week into the 2019 season, but the drag numbers so far are among the lowest recorded in the last calendar year. With apologies for gory math, the current 2019 season average drag coefficient (the red line) would be below the 95 percent credible interval (the shaded area) for about nine-tenths of the 2018 season. (I used a Bayesian Random Walk model implemented in INLA to calculate these credible intervals, averaging the drag numbers in each game and adjusting for park.)

There were only a handful of six-day stretches in 2018 that had drag numbers below what we're seeing now, and most were in late June and early July. All of this means that 2019's data so far is quite a bit different than what we saw through most of last year.

These drag coefficients factor out the effects of temperature and air density, so they aren't a product of April cold. However, the numbers could be deceptive if the radars used to track pitches have changed from year to year. I consulted with some experts within baseball who were not aware of any specific modifications to the radar this year that could produce this pattern, but it's an important caveat of which to be aware.

On the one hand, it's only been six days, and we don't quite have the statistical basis to say that these drag coefficients are unprecedented compared to 2018. On the other hand, we've witnessed about 5,000 fastballs so far this season, so it's not as if our sample size is small. At least so far, the baseball has played like it's much more aerodynamic than it was last year. In fact, the current drag coefficient is really only comparable to 2017, when the baseballs were more aerodynamic than they had been in at least a decade.

It's not just fancy radar tracking indicating that the baseball is flying through the air more easily. The current number of home runs per game (as of this writing) is the highest it's been since the heady days of 2017, the year that teams and players broke dinger-related records everywhere you looked. That's especially remarkable considering that we're in what is typically the coldest part of the regular season, when lower temperatures and higher winds tend to suppress offense and keep balls in the air within the park. Comparing only from April to April, this year's rate of home runs per fly ball is even a little bit higher than it was in 2017.

With that said, the current measurements are no guarantee that 2019 will be another year of record-shattering homer hitting. The trouble with the drag measurements is that they are not consistent from June to August, from week to week, or even sometimes from day to day. Whether because of natural manufacturing variation or differences in the underlying supplies of cowhide and thread that go into the baseballs, drag has a tendency to fluctuate up and down over the course of a year. So the homers that fly in the first week of April wouldn't necessarily clear the fence a week later.

It's possible that this one-week drop in drag coefficient subsides and the baseball returns to its 2018 levels. On the other hand, it's almost equally probable that the ball becomes even more slippery and flies ever farther. Either way, it's clear that the baseball's air resistance is something to keep an eye on for the remainder of the 2019 season.

—*Robert Arthur is an author of Baseball Prospectus.*

The Moral Hazard of Playing It Safe

Craig Goldstein

This article originally appeared at Baseball Prospectus on August 6, 2019.

A couple days prior to the trade deadline, amidst a sea of tranquility posing as the lead up to the trade deadline, Bob Nightengale took to Twitter. Nightengale, who was probably wearing his pants backwards at the time, tweeted that MLB GMs were coming around on the idea that the unified trade deadline should be moved back from July 31 to August 15, so they could better assess their positions in the standings and whether they should buy or sell. To which I said:

This might strike some as reductive and churlish. And it might be that, but it isn't really wrong, either. Jeff Quinton wrote a great piece discussing the environmental factors that enable front offices to avoid risk without upsetting the apple cart within their own fanbases. I don't believe that it goes far enough, however. His article gives us the proper framework through which to understand why these behaviors have been allowed to seep into front offices throughout the league. Understanding the reasons behind these actions are different from excusing them, though, and GMs should not be let off the hook for their non-competitive approach to the trade deadline (much less the offseason).

⚾ ⚾ ⚾

It's fair to say that fans as a group have rarely, if ever, been pro-player. It is also fair to say that in the time during and following the Moneyball revolution, the pendulum swung from fans who cared intensely about winning in the moment (and thus might be intolerant of a rebuilding approach) to fans who supported building a team that could compete throughout multiple seasons, viewing the playoffs as a crapshoot, with the thought that getting multiple bites at the apple was a better approach than taking a bigger bite in any one season.

There's nothing wrong with that approach, and I still find merit in that argument. However, it seems that the pendulum has swung too far in that direction. Teams are overvaluing some of the individual factors that make themselves long-term contenders rather than attempting to seize a championship when given the opportunity. It's a difficult needle to thread.

And surely, they (and those in similar positions) would have liked another two weeks to clarify where they stand so as to better marshal their resources. We've all asked for a few more minutes when staring at a menu. But all of these GMs and front office personnel are where they are to make difficult decisions. They have proprietary data and internal analysts dedicated to understanding their position relative to the rest of the league, and how any move in the here and now impacts their long-term vision. To complain (if that report is accurate) that over half the season is not enough to properly assess their season is bullshit of the highest order. Move the deadline, and you'd simply have increasingly discounted trade offers because teams would be acquiring even less control of anyone they're acquiring, rental or not.

Major league front offices are behaving like the managers they lampooned two decades ago. They're effectively sacrificing a runner to second in the ninth inning—not because it's the correct move, but rather because it is safe. It used to be that the phrase "moral hazard" was used to describe general managers who made ill-fated, short-sighted decisions aimed at locking in wins and securing their jobs at the expense of their team's future. Now, general managers are guilty of committing moral hazards in the opposite direction, playing it utterly safe and terrified of becoming scapegoats.

In lieu of bold action, they opt to pussyfoot around a current window of contention, choosing instead to play the long game and stack up years of control like they're blocks in a game of Jenga. GMs pass on signing quality players in free agency because the back-end of the deal might look bad, and because they might be able to squeeze out 70 percent of the production from a player who costs a tenth as much. That's a safer investment, too, because it's also hard to prove a negative—it's impossible to prove that Manny Machado would make the Mets a playoff team in 2019-2020, but it's easy to say that the back half of Robinson Cano's contract sucks. Owners, who rule over GM's jobs, are also humans with human brain processes that will always make the so-called albatross contract uglier than the road not taken.

These days, GMs are remembered for the bad deals they make and the surplus value they generate, not the acquisition of expensive, necessary talents that meet their market worth (or fall slightly short while still providing significant on-field value). And front offices know that one or two expensive misfires can cost them their jobs, no matter how many good deals they make.

No front office exemplifies this ethos more than the Toronto Blue Jays. General Manager Ross Atkins had this to say following the Blue Jays underwhelming trade deadline:

This is by no means the first time that an executive will cite years of control to justify their actions, which is often just another way of saying "don't look at what we got, look at how much we got of it." Atkins touts quantity to elide the discussion of quality—either, that of the players acquired, or those given up. Remember: the other teams presumably value years of control, too.

Atkins also had some thoughts to offer regarding free agents back in early 2018:

This ignores, of course, whether the player can create enough value in the front end of a contract to justify the longer term of a deal, and the decline that often occurs in the back end. It also ignores whether the player can fill a need the team requires and put them in a position to compete for and win a championship. But as teams seemingly avoid contention at all, where they might end up having to consider and later justify some of these tough decisions, we still see risk-averse approaches.

Anthony Fenech's article on two trades that recently extended GM Al Avila didn't make got at this issue rather well:

> Passing on those deals was defensible: Both players had yet to break out and trading [Michael] Fulmer—a pitcher who appeared to be a future ace, no matter his injury concerns—would have taken serious gumption, opening Avila up to strong criticism.

Avoiding strong criticism is something each of us can understand as a motivation, but the avoidance of criticism only matters if that criticism is valid. In Fulmer's case, shoving his injury concerns aside affects not only the years that the team controls him (he is currently missing a full season due to Tommy John surgery) but also the quality of those seasons, as his knee and elbow injuries combined to dampen his effectiveness even when healthy enough to pitch. But it was easy to present the then-current image of Fulmer as a top of the rotation pitcher who the team had under its domain for the next five seasons as something to build around. The status quo isn't nearly as often second-guessed as a decision that disrupts it.

⚾ ⚾ ⚾

MLB GMs are risk-averse to a fault. They are ivy-educated and consulting firm-approved, and yet they can't seem to avoid leaving wins on the table in their all-consuming lust for a non-existent $/WAR championship. They are supposed to zig when everyone else zags, and not merely pay lip service to the idea of zigging through a calculated PR plan built on convincing the fan base their approach is novel when it actually apes most of their competitors. Instead they've become far more concerned with making safe, accepted-by-the-new-common-wisdom decisions, such that our prior understanding of what a moral hazard is has become inverted.

I can't blame them entirely, and not only because of the reasons that Quinton illuminated in his article, but also because of the damage wrought by the introduction of the second wild card (WC2) spot. MLB's desire to have more teams in playoff contention has sparked anti-competitive behavior. Teams know now that they do not need to swing big as they assemble their roster because there is a good chance that a mediocre team can either catch fire and capture a division, or muddle along until they back into the WC2.

Simultaneously, the one-game playoff has neutered the WC1, putting an entire season on the flip of a coin like some sort of baseball-obsessed Anton Chigurh. While the one-game playoff makes sense as a way to increase the value of winning a division, it also means that if a front office doesn't like its chances of overcoming a behemoth like the Dodgers or Astros in the offseason, they have few incentives to chase glory. Similarly, the relative inaction in the NL Central at the trade deadline—despite a wide open division—can be explained by the idea that any high-variance investment could still result in only a wild card (or worse) result, given the mere two months left in the season to make an impact.

⚾   ⚾   ⚾

As stated at the top, we should not confuse reasons for excuses. The implementation of the second wild card is just one of many environmental factors that influence how each front office operates. I am convinced that it is one of the larger factors, but I am also convinced that organizations need to shed the yoke of "efficiency at all costs" so that they can instead pursue competition, as the spirit of the game intends. Until they do, we're all deadline losers.

—*Craig Goldstein is an author of Baseball Prospectus.*

Index of Names

Adams, Austin 40
Altavilla, Dan 42
Alvarado, Elvis 90
Bautista, Gerson 44
Beckham, Tim 18
Bins, Carter 88
Bishop, Braden 88, 103
Bradford, Chasen 90
Brennan, Brandon 46
Campbell, Isaiah 102
Carasiti, Matt 90
Carlson, Sam 102
Casetta-Stubbs, Damon 104
Cortes Jr., Nestor 48
Crawford, J.P. 20
Crismatt, Nabil 90
Delaplane, Sam 90
Dunn, Justin 50, 96
Edwards Jr., Carl 52
Festa, Matt 90
Filia, Eric 74
Fletcher, Aaron 90
Fraley, Jake 75, 100
Gerber, Joey 90, 103
Gilbert, Logan 82, 94
Gonzales, Marco 54
Gordon, Dee 22
Graveman, Kendall 83
Grotz, Zac 56
Guilbeau, Taylor 58
Haniger, Mitch 24

Hirano, Yoshihisa 60
Kelenic, Jarred 76, 93
Kikuchi, Yusei 62
Kirby, George 84, 97
Lewis, Kyle 26, 100
Long, Shed 28
Lopes, Tim 88
Magill, Matt 64
Margevicius, Nick 66
Marte, Noelvi 98
Mills, Wyatt 90, 104
Misiewicz, Anthony 90
Moore, Andrew 90
Moore, Dylan 88
Murfee, Penn 90
Murphy, Tom 30
Newsome, Ljay 90, 102
Nola, Austin 32
O'Keefe, Brian 88
Raleigh, Cal 77, 101
Ramirez, Yohan 90
Rodriguez, Julio 78, 94
Sadzeck, Connor 90
Sanchez, Ricardo 90
Seager, Kyle 34
Sheffield, Justus 68, 99
Shenton, Austin 104
Siri, Jose 79
Smith, Mallex 36
Swanson, Erik 70
Then, Juan 85, 97

Seattle Mariners 2020

Thompson-Williams, Dom 88
Tuivailala, Sam 72
Valdez, Phillip 91
Vizcaino, Arodys 91
Vogelbach, Daniel 38
Walker, Taijuan 86

Walton, Donnie 80
Warren, Art 87, 103
White, Evan 81, 95
Williamson, Brandon 91, 101
Wisdom, Patrick 88